Mammals
of # Georgia

Field Guide

by Stan Tekiela

Adventure Publications, Inc.
Cambridge, Minnesota

To naturalists everywhere who have committed to spreading the word of conservation.

ACKNOWLEDGMENTS

A heartfelt thanks to Rick and Nora Bowers, who greatly helped me obtain many of the photos for this book. Special thanks to the National Wildlife Refuge System and the many public and private state and local agencies for stewarding the lands that are critical to the wild mammals we love so much.

Edited by Sandy Livoti

Cover and book design by Jonathan Norberg

Silhouettes, tracks and range maps by Anthony Hertzel

Cover photo: Gray Fox by Stan Tekiela
See pages 330-331 for photo credits by photographer and page number.

10 9 8 7 6 5 4 3 2 1

Copyright 2011 by Stan Tekiela
Published by Adventure Publications, Inc.
820 Cleveland St. S
Cambridge, MN 55008
1-800-678-7006
www.adventurepublications.net
All rights reserved
Printed in China

ISBN: 978-1-59193-305-2

TABLE OF CONTENTS

Introduction

The Mammals

Mice & Rats

Squirrels

GEORGIA'S MAMMALS

Georgia is a great place for wildlife watchers! This state is one of the few places to see magnificent mammals, such as the elusive Cougar, along with many interesting animals such as the Nine-banded Armadillo. While West Indian Manatees swim in the rivers of Georgia, Bobcats thrive in nearly all habitats across the state. No matter where you may be in Georgia, there is a wide variety of mammals to see and enjoy.

Mammals of Georgia Field Guide is an easy-to-use field guide to help the curious nature lover identify all species of mammals found in Georgia. It is an all-photographic guide just for Georgia, featuring full-color images of animals in their habitats. It is one in a series of unique field guides for Georgia that includes birds, mammals and wildflowers.

WHAT IS A MAMMAL?

The first mammals appeared in the late Triassic Period, about 200 million years ago. These ancient mammals were small, lacked diversity and looked nothing like our current-day mammals. During the following Jurassic Period, mammal size and diversity started to increase. Mammals generally started to appear more like today's mammals in the Cenozoic Era, which occurred after the mass extinction of dinosaurs, about 60 million years ago.

Today, modern mammals are a large group of animals that includes nearly 5,500 species around the world, with more than 400 species in North America. Here in Georgia we have 83 species, most native to the state. They range from the Least Shrew, a tiny mammal no larger than a human thumb, to the very large and majestic American Bison, which can grow to a length of 12 feet (3.7 m) and weigh up to 2,000 pounds (900 kg). Georgia also has non-native (exotic) animals such as the Nutria, Fallow Deer and Wild Hog.

All mammals have some common traits or characteristics. Mammals have a backbone (vertebra) and are warm-blooded (endothermic). In endothermic animals, the process of eating and

breaking down food in the digestive tract produces heat, which keeps the animal warm even on cold winter nights. Except during periods of hibernation or torpor, the body temperature of mammals stays within a narrow range, just as it does in people. Body temperature is controlled with rapid, open-mouthed breathing known as panting, by shunting blood flow to or away from areas with networks of blood vessels, such as ears, for cooling or conserving heat. When blood flows through vessels that are close to the surface of skin, heat is released and the body cools. When blood flows away from the surface of skin, heat is conserved.

Most mammals are covered with a thick coat of fur or hair. Fur is critical for survival and needs to be kept clean and in good condition. In some animals, such as the Northern River Otter, the fur is so thick it keeps the underlying skin warm and dry even while swimming. Just as birds must preen their feathers to maintain good health, animals spend hours each day licking and "combing" or grooming their fur. You can easily observe this grooming behavior in your pet cat or dog.

Mammals share several other characteristics. All females bear live young and suckle their babies with milk produced from the mammary glands. Mother's milk provides young mammals with total nourishment during the first part of their lives. Also, mammals have sound-conducting bones in their middle ears. These bones give animals the ability to hear as people do and, in many cases, hear much better.

Mammals are diphyodont, meaning they have two sets of teeth. There are milk or deciduous teeth, which fall out, and permanent teeth, also known as adult teeth. Adult teeth usually consist of incisors, canines, premolars and molars, but these categories can be highly variable in each mammal family. Teeth are often used to classify or group mammals into families in the same manner as the bill of a bird is used to classify or group birds into families.

Reproduction in mammals can be complex and difficult to understand. Many mammals have delayed implantation, which means

after the egg and sperm have joined (impregnation), the resulting embryo remains in a suspended state until becoming implanted in the uterine wall. The delay time can be anywhere from a few days to weeks or months. An animal that becomes stressed from lack of food will pass the embryo out of the reproductive tract, and no pregnancy occurs. Conversely, well-fed mothers may have twins or even triplets. Bats and some other species store sperm in the reproductive tract over winter. Impregnation is delayed until spring, and implantation occurs right after impregnation. This process is known as delayed impregnation.

Most mammals are nocturnal, secretive and don't make a lot of noise, so they tend to go unnoticed. Signs of mammals, such as tracks or scat, are often more commonly seen than the actual animal. However, if you spend some time in the right habitat at the right time of day, your chances of seeing mammals will increase.

IDENTIFICATION STEP-BY-STEP

Fortunately, most large mammals are easy to identify and are not confused with other species. This is not the case, however, with small mammals such as mice or voles. Small animals, while plentiful, can be a challenge to correctly identify because they often have only minor differences in teeth or internal organs and bones.

This field guide is organized by families, starting with small animals, such as shrews and mice, and ending with large mammals such as bison and dolphins. Within each family section, the animals are in size order from small to large.

Each mammal has four to six pages of color photos and text, with a silhouette of the animal illustrated on the first description page. Each silhouette is located in a quick-compare tab in the upper right corner. Decide which animal group you are seeing, use the quick-compare tabs to locate the pages for that group, then compare the photos with your animal. If you aren't sure of the identity, the text on description pages explains identifying features that may or may not be easily seen. The first description

page for each species also has a compare section with notes about similar species in this field guide. Other pertinent details and the naturalist facts in Stan's Notes will help you correctly identify your mammal in question. Photos of other species will help you identify all of the mammals of Georgia.

Thus, every effort has been made to provide relevant identification information including range maps, which can help you eliminate some choices. Colored areas of the maps show where a species can be seen, but not the density of the species. While ranges are accurately depicted, they change on an ongoing basis due to a variety of factors. Please use the maps as intended–as a general guide only.

Finally, if you already know the name of your animal, simply use the index to quickly find the page and learn more about the species from the text and photos.

For many people, an animal's track or silhouette is all they might see of an animal. However, tracks in mud or sand and silhouettes are frequently difficult to identify. Special quick-compare pages, beginning on page 14, are a great place to start the identification process. These pages group similar kinds of animals and tracks side by side for easy comparison. For example, all hoofed animals, such as deer, are grouped in one section and all dog-like animals are grouped in another. Within the groupings, silhouettes and tracks are illustrated in relative size from small to large. This format allows you to compare one silhouette or track shape and size with another that is similarly shaped and sized. When you don't know whether you're seeing the silhouette or track of a coyote or wolf, a deer or other similar species, use the quick-compare pages for quick and easy reference.

To begin, find the group that your unknown silhouette or track looks similar to and start comparing. Since each group has relatively few animals, it won't take long to narrow your choices. A ruler can be handy to measure your track and compare it with the size given in the book. To confirm the identity of the silhou-

ette or track and for more detailed information about the animal, refer to the description pages for the number of toes, length of stride and other distinguishing characteristics.

TAXONOMY OF GEORGIA'S MAMMALS

Biologists classify mammals based on their ancestry and physical characteristics. Georgia mammals are grouped into 10 scientific orders. Charts with the scientific classification (taxonomy) are shown on the Appendix, pages 316-325. Each of the 10 charts starts with one of the orders and shows all scientific families and mammals in that particular order.

CAUTION

Hunting, trapping, possessing and other activities involving animals are regulated by the Georgia Department of Natural Resources. You should familiarize yourself with the laws and seasons before doing any kill trapping, live trapping and hunting.

As interesting as all of these animals are, resist any temptation to capture any animal for a pet. Wild animals, even babies, never make good pets. Wild animals often have specific dietary and habitat requirements that rarely can be duplicated in a captive situation, and many will not survive. In many cases, capturing animals for pets is also illegal. This practice not only diminishes the population, it reduces the possibility for future reproduction. Furthermore, some animals are uncommon in Georgia, and their populations can be even more quickly depleted.

Live trapping of animals in an attempt to rid your yard of them rarely works. The removal of an animal from its habitat creates a void that is quickly filled with a neighboring animal or its offspring, recreating the original situation. Moreover, an unfortunate animal that is live trapped and moved to a new location often cannot find a habitat with an adequate food supply, shelter or a territory that is not already occupied. Animals that have been moved often die from exposure to weather, are struck by vehicles

while crossing roads or killed by resident animals. With habitat ranges growing smaller every year, removing just one animal can have a direct impact on the local population of a species. We can all learn to live with our wild animals with just a few modifications to our yards and attitudes. Observe and record animals with your camera, but leave them where they belong–in the wild.

Encounters with wildlife often involve injured or orphaned animals. Many well-intentioned people with little or no resources or knowledge of what is needed try to care for such animals. Injured or orphaned animals deserve the best care, so please do the right thing if you find one and turn it over to a licensed professional wildlife rehabilitator. Information about wildlife rehabilitation in Georgia is listed in the resource section of this field guide. The rehabilitation staff may often be able to give you updates on the condition of an animal you bring in and even when it is released. When you take an animal to a rehab center, you might also want to consider making a monetary donation to help cover the costs involved for its care.

Enjoy the Wild Mammals!

Stan

Body length measurements
do not include tail.

Average size of the smallest and largest of this group compared to an 8" hand.

Silhouettes are in proportion by average body length. Tracks are in proportion by average largest foot. Front track is on the left and hind is on the right.

1⅞"
Least Shrew
pg. 37

⅛"   ⅜"

2" 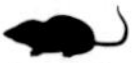
Masked Shrew
pg. 41

⅛"   ⅜"

2½" 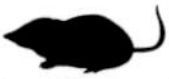
Southeastern Shrew
pg. 53

⅜"   ½"

2½" 
Meadow Jumping Mouse pg. 81

½"   1¼"

3½" 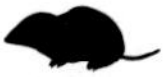
Northern Short-tailed Shrew pg. 61

⅜"   ⅝"

3½" 
Southern Red-backed Vole pg. 137

½"   ¾"

3½" 
Woodland Jumping Mouse pg. 97

½"   1¼"

4" 
Cotton Mouse
pg. 113

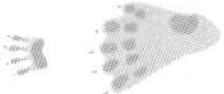

¾"   1"

4⅛" 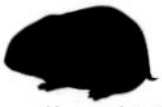
Woodland Vole
pg. 141

¼"   ⅝"

4½" 
Water Shrew
pg. 65

¼"   ⅜"

14

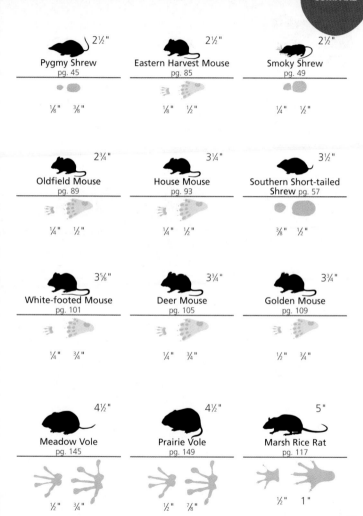

2½"
Pygmy Shrew
pg. 45

⅛"   ⅜"

2½"
Eastern Harvest Mouse
pg. 85

⅛"   ½"

2½"
Smoky Shrew
pg. 49

¼"   ½"

2¾"
Oldfield Mouse
pg. 89

¼"   ½"

3¼"
House Mouse
pg. 93

¼"   ½"

3½"
**Southern Short-tailed
Shrew** pg. 57

⅜"   ½"

3⅝"
White-footed Mouse
pg. 101

¼"   ¾"

3¾"
Deer Mouse
pg. 105

¼"   ¾"

3¾"
Golden Mouse
pg. 109

½"   ¾"

4½"
Meadow Vole
pg. 145

½"   ¾"

4½"
Prairie Vole
pg. 149

½"   ⅞"

5"
Marsh Rice Rat
pg. 117

½"   1"

15

Body length measurements
do not include tail.

Average size of the smallest and
largest of this group compared to
an 8" hand.

Silhouettes are in proportion by
average body length. Tracks are
in proportion by average largest
foot. Front track is on the left and
hind is on the right.

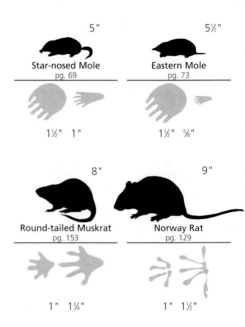

5"

Star-nosed Mole
pg. 69

1½"   1"

5½"

Eastern Mole
pg. 73

1½"   ⅝"

8"

Round-tailed Muskrat
pg. 153

1"   1¾"

9"

Norway Rat
pg. 129

1"   1½"

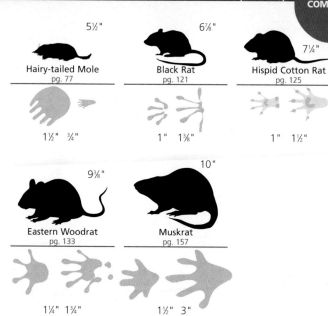

5½"

Hairy-tailed Mole
pg. 77

1½"   ¾"

6⅞"

Black Rat
pg. 121

1"   1⅜"

7¼"

Hispid Cotton Rat
pg. 125

1"   1½"

9⅜"

Eastern Woodrat
pg. 133

1¼"   1¾"

10"

Muskrat
pg. 157

1½"   3"

Body length measurements
do not include tail.

Average size of the smallest and
largest of this group compared to
an 8" hand.

Silhouettes are in proportion
to each other by average body
length.

1¾"
Little Brown Bat
pg. 172
no tracks

2⅛"
Eastern Pipistrelle
pg. 172
no tracks

2⅜"
Brazilian Free-tailed Bat
pg. 172
no tracks

2½"
Big Brown Bat
pg. 169
no tracks

3"
Hoary Bat
pg. 173
no tracks

3⅛"
Gray Myotis
pg. 173
no tracks

3½"
Southeastern Bat
pg. 173
no tracks

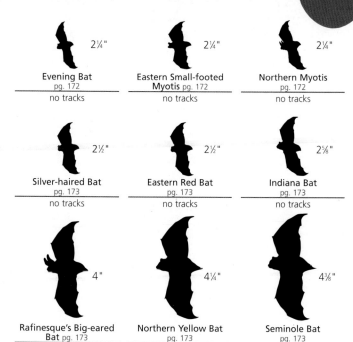

2¼"

Evening Bat
pg. 172
no tracks

2¼"

**Eastern Small-footed
Myotis** pg. 172
no tracks

2¼"

Northern Myotis
pg. 172
no tracks

2½"

Silver-haired Bat
pg. 173
no tracks

2½"

Eastern Red Bat
pg. 173
no tracks

2⅝"

Indiana Bat
pg. 173
no tracks

4"

**Rafinesque's Big-eared
Bat** pg. 173
no tracks

4¼"

Northern Yellow Bat
pg. 173
no tracks

4⅜"

Seminole Bat
pg. 173
no tracks

19

Body length measurements
do not include tail.

Average size of the smallest and
largest of this group compared to
a 6' human.

Silhouettes are in proportion by
average body length. Tracks are
in proportion by average largest
foot. Front track is on the left and
hind is on the right.

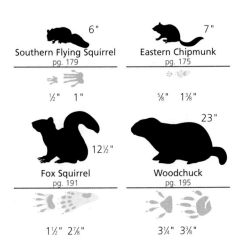

6"
Southern Flying Squirrel
pg. 179

½"   1"

7"
Eastern Chipmunk
pg. 175

⅝"   1⅜"

12½"
Fox Squirrel
pg. 191

1½"   2⅞"

23"
Woodchuck
pg. 195

3¼"   3⅜"

8"

Red Squirrel
pg. 183

¾"   1½"

 9½"

Eastern Gray Squirrel
pg. 187

1"   2¼"

 11"

**Southeastern Pocket
Gopher** pg. 199

1¼"   ¾"

Body length measurements
do not include tail.

Average size of the smallest and
largest of this group compared to
a 6' human.

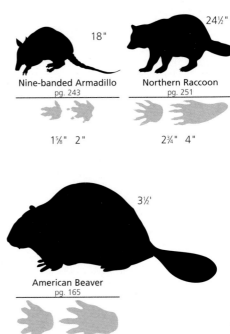

18"

Nine-banded Armadillo
pg. 243

1⅝"   2"

24½"

Northern Raccoon
pg. 251

2¾"   4"

3½'

American Beaver
pg. 165

3"   5"

Silhouettes are in proportion by
average body length. Tracks are
in proportion by average largest
foot. Front track is on the left and
hind is on the right.

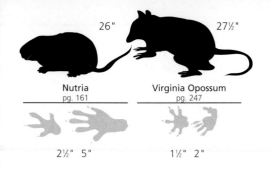

26"

27½"

Nutria
pg. 161

Virginia Opossum
pg. 247

2½" 5"

1½" 2"

Body length measurements
do not include tail.

Average size of the smallest and
largest of this group compared to
a 6' human.

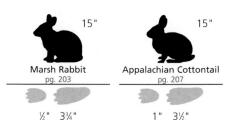

	15"		15"
Marsh Rabbit pg. 203		**Appalachian Cottontail** pg. 207	
½" 3¾"		1" 3½"	

Body length measurements
do not include tail.

Average size of the smallest and
largest of this group compared to
a 6' human.

Silhouettes are in proportion by
average body length. Tracks are
in proportion by average largest
foot. Front track is on the left and
hind is on the right.

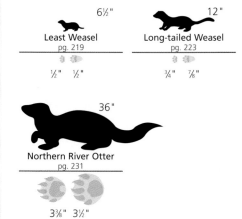

	6½"		12"
Least Weasel pg. 219		**Long-tailed Weasel** pg. 223	
½" ½"		¾" ⅞"	

36"

Northern River Otter
pg. 231

3⅜" 3½"

16"

Eastern Cottontail
pg. 211

20"

Swamp Rabbit
pg. 215

1"   3½"

½"   4½"

14"

Eastern Spotted Skunk
pg. 235

17"

Mink
pg. 227

22"

Striped Skunk
pg. 239

1"   1¼"

1½"   2⅝"

1⅜"   2¾"

Body length measurements
do not include tail.

Average size of the smallest and
largest of this group compared to
a 6' human.

23"

Gray Fox
pg. 255

1½" 1⅜"

23"

Red Fox
pg. 259

2" 1⅞"

Body length measurements
do not include tail.

Average size of the smallest and
largest of this group compared to
a 6' human.

Silhouettes are in proportion by
average body length. Tracks are
in proportion by average largest
foot. Front track is on the left and
hind is on the right.

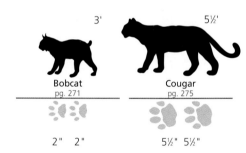

3'

Bobcat
pg. 271

2" 2"

5½'

Cougar
pg. 275

5½" 5½"

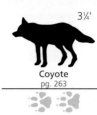

3¼'

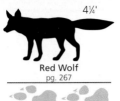

4¼'

Coyote
pg. 263

Red Wolf
pg. 267

2¼" 2⅛"

6" 5⅞"

Body length measurements do not include tail.

Average size of the smallest and largest of this group compared to a 6' human.

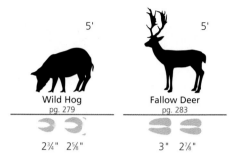

5'

Wild Hog
pg. 279

5'

Fallow Deer
pg. 283

2¾"   2⅝"

3"   2⅞"

Body length measurements do not include tail.

Average size of the smallest and largest of this group compared to a 6' human.

Silhouettes are in proportion by average body length. Tracks are in proportion by average largest foot. Front track is on the left and hind is on the right.

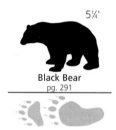

5¼'

Black Bear
pg. 291

4"   8"

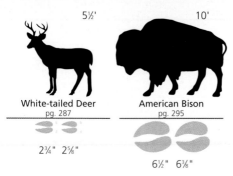

White-tailed Deer
pg. 287

American Bison
pg. 295

5½'

10'

2¾" 2⅝"

6½" 6⅜"

Body length measurements
include the tail.

Average size of the smallest and
largest of this group compared to
a 6' human.

Silhouettes are in proportion by
average body length.

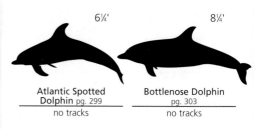

6¼'

8¼'

**Atlantic Spotted
Dolphin** pg. 299

no tracks

Bottlenose Dolphin
pg. 303

no tracks

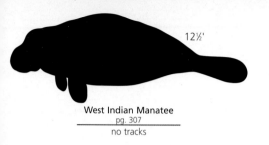

12½'

West Indian Manatee
pg. 307
no tracks

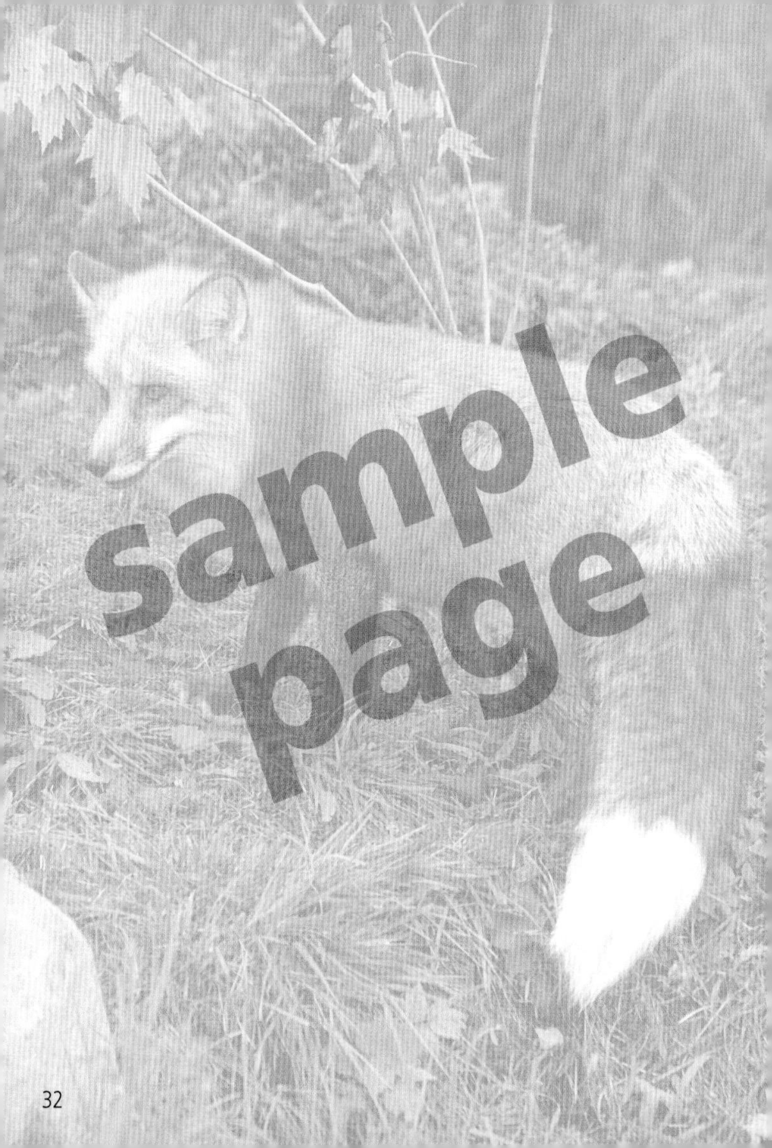

FORMER
RANGE

Group Color Tab

Common Name

Range Map *Scientific name* Shape

Family: common family name (scientific family name)

Size: (L) average length or range of length of body from head to rump; for marine, range of length from head to tail; (T) average length or range of length of tail; (H) average height or range of height to top of back

Weight: average weight or range of weight; may include (M) male and (F) female weights

Description: brief description of the mammal; may include color morphs, seasonal variations or differences between male and female

Origin/Age: native or non-native to Georgia or the waters off the coast; average life span in the wild

Compare: notes about other species that look similar and the pages on which they can be found; may include extra information to help identify

Habitat: environment where the animal is seen (e.g., wetlands, scrublands, fields, prairies, forests)

Home: description of nest, burrow or den; may include other related information

Food: herbivore, carnivore, insectivore, omnivore or ichthyophagous; what the animal eats most of the time; may include other related information

Sounds: vocalization or other noises the animal creates; may include variant sounds or other information

Breeding: mating season; length of gestation

Young: number of offspring born per year and when; may include description or birth weight

Sample page

33

summer coat

winter coat

silver morph   dark morph

scat

Signs: evidence that the animal was there or is near; may include a description of scat; other comments

Activity: diurnal, nocturnal, crepuscular; other comments

Tracks: forepaw and hind paw or hoof size and shape, largest size first; pattern of tracks; description of prints, which may include tail drag mark or stride; other comments

Tracks and Pattern

Stan's Notes: Interesting gee-whiz natural history information. This can be something to look or listen for, or something to help positively identify the animal such as remarkable features. May include additional photos to illustrate juveniles, nests, unique behaviors and other key characteristics.

den entrance

kits

Similar species on next page (bat species only) 35

Least Shrew
Cryptotis parva

Family: Shrews (Soricidae)

Size: L 1½-2¼" (4-5.5 cm); T ½-¾" (1-2 cm)

Weight: ⅛-¼ oz. (4-7 g)

Description: Mostly brown above, but fur can be gray. Lighter belly. Pointed snout. Tiny dark eyes. Short tail, never more than twice as long as the hind foot. Small pink feet. Ears barely visible.

Origin/Age: native; 1-2 years

Compare: The Southern Short-tailed Shrew (pg. 57) and Northern Short-tailed Shrew (pg. 61) are darker overall with larger bodies, but similar length tails. Smaller than Southeastern Shrew (pg. 53) and has a shorter tail. Masked Shrew (pg. 41) is larger, with a longer snout and tail.

Habitat: fields, grasslands, meadows, shrubby areas

Home: chamber in an underground burrow, nest made with dried leaves and grasses

Food: insectivore, carnivore; beetles, crickets, spiders, grasshoppers, slugs, earthworms, snails, small mammals

Sounds: inconsequential; sharp squeaks and high-pitched whistles can be heard from up to 2' (61 cm) away

Breeding: Mar-Nov mating; 21-23 days gestation

Young: 1-6 offspring several times per year; born naked with eyes closed, weaned at about 3 weeks

Signs: partially eaten insects near the burrow entrance; extremely tiny, dark scat, widely scattered

Activity: nocturnal, diurnal; may be more active during the day in summer, when nights are shorter

Tracks: hind paw ¼-½" (.6-1 cm) long, forepaw slightly smaller; 1 set of 4 tracks, but prints are so close together they appear to be 1 track; 4 prints together are 1 square inch (6.5 sq. cm), often lacks a tail drag mark due to its short tail

Stan's Notes: One of Georgia's least studied shrew species, thus not much is known about its biology. Range in the United States is widespread, from Minnesota down to Texas, east to Georgia and up the entire East coast, excluding New England.

Sometimes called Bee Shrew because it supposedly lives in beehives; however, this has never been studied or widely reported and may be a reference to the animal's small size. It has been reported to take up residency in a beehive while eating the bees that occupy it.

Hunts for invertebrates by probing through leaf litter with its nose, smelling for prey. Often feeds only on the internal organs of large insects. Subdues prey by capturing and biting off the head, which makes it easier to get to internal organs. Like other shrews, it eats nearly its own body weight in food each day. When food is abundant it will cache some for later consumption.

While most other shrew species are solitary, Least Shrew appears to be more social, with many individuals sharing one nest. It is thought that owls, particularly Barn Owls, are its major predators. In one study, Least Shrews made up 41 percent of the diet of one Barn Owl pair. In another pair, Least Shrews made up 73 percent of the diet.

Masked Shrew
Sorex cinereus

Family: Shrews (Soricidae)

Size: L 1¾-2¼" (4.5-5.5 cm); T 1-2" (2.5-5 cm)

Weight: ¼ oz. (7 g)

Description: Overall brown-to-gray fur, with lighter gray-to-white belly. Very long, pointed snout. Tiny dark eyes. Ears slightly visible. Long hairy tail, brown above and lighter below with a dark tuft at tip.

Origin/Age: native; 1-2 years

Compare: The small size, brown color and long tail of the Masked Shrew help distinguish it from the other shrews in Georgia. The Pygmy Shrew (pg. 45) is slightly smaller and has a shorter tail.

Habitat: meadows, forests, willow thickets

Home: nest, 4-6" (10-15 cm) wide, made of leaves and grasses, under a log or rock

Food: insectivore, carnivore; insects, ants, slugs, spiders, earthworms, small mammals such as mice

Sounds: inconsequential; sharp squeaks and high-pitched whistles

Breeding: spring to autumn mating; 18 days gestation

Young: 5-7 offspring 2-3 times per year; young are born naked with eyes closed, eyes open at 17-19 days, weaned at about 20 days, on own within days of being weaned, young born in fall are less likely to survive due to lack of food

41

Signs: tiny tunnels or runways in freshly dug soil; shrew is rarely, if ever, seen

Activity: diurnal, nocturnal; active under snow in winter

Tracks: hind paw ¼-½" (.6-1 cm) long, forepaw slightly smaller; 1 set of 4 tracks, but prints are so close together they appear as 1 track; 4 prints together are 1 square inch (6.5 sq. cm), sometimes has a slight tail drag mark

Stan's Notes: This very secretive, solitary animal is rarely seen because of its underground lifestyle. Also called Cinereus Shrew, it is one of the smallest mammals in Georgia. It is also one of the most widespread mammals in North America, ranging all across Canada and Alaska and the northern-tiered states, reaching as far south as Georgia.

Its long pointed snout is characteristic of all 33 species of shrews seen in North America. Gives off a strong musky odor, which makes it unattractive to large mammalian predators, but the scent does not seem to deter birds of prey such as owls and hawks. Heart rate will race to as many as 1,200 beats per minute when it is excited. Can die from fright when captured.

Has little body mass due to its small size, so it must feed nearly every hour to keep warm or starve to death. Moves constantly, darting about to find food. Often eats more than its own body weight daily in worms, slugs and beetles. Will kill mice, which are larger than itself. Seeks dormant insects and larvae in winter. Does not hibernate.

A desirable animal to have around your home and yard because it eats many harmful insects and keeps populations of mice in check. Does not transmit rabies and is not harmful to humans.

Pygmy Shrew
Sorex hoyi

Family: Shrews (Soricidae)

Size: L 2-3" (5-7.5 cm); T 1" (2.5 cm)

Weight: ⅛ oz. (4 g)

Description: Brown to gray above, sometimes coppery brown. Belly is light gray to silver. Long pointed snout. Ears hidden by fur. Tiny dark eyes. A long hairy tail, dark brown above and paler below, about 40-50 percent of total length.

Origin/Age: native; 1 year

Compare: The Southern Short-tailed Shrew (pg. 57) and Northern Short-tailed Shrew (pg. 61) are larger, much darker and have shorter tails. Consider the range when identifying this species.

Habitat: coniferous forests, bogs, brushy fields

Home: nest made from dried plant material, 2 openings, under a log or stump; builds several nests

Food: insectivore, carnivore; beetles, crickets, small grasshoppers, spiders, worms, small amphibians

Sounds: inconsequential; sharp squeaks and high-pitched whistles

Breeding: Mar-Sep mating; 18-20 days gestation

Young: 2-8 offspring 1-2 times per year; born naked with eyes closed

Signs: multiple round nests made of plant material with surface runways leading to and from nests

Activity: nocturnal, diurnal; slightly more active at night

Tracks: hind paw ⅜" (.9 cm) long, forepaw slightly smaller; 1 set of 4 tracks, but prints are so close together they appear as 1 track; 4 prints together are 1 square inch (6.5 sq. cm), sometimes has a tail drag mark

Stan's Notes: This is one of the smallest and rarest mammals in Georgia and North America, never seen in great abundance. Known to inhabit only those areas where coniferous trees are most plentiful. Range extends from New England to Minnesota and northwest across Canada to Alaska, and also south, down the Appalachian Mountains, touching the northern edge of Georgia. Pygmy Shrews in Alaska and Canada are much larger than those in Georgia, with up to a 2 gram difference in weight.

Tolerates a wide variety of habitats from wet to dry and cold to warm, regardless of the vegetative type. Usually associated with a specific vegetative variety including trees such as Paper Birch, Jack Pine, hazelnut, aspen and alder.

Not much is known about the Pygmy Shrew. Runs with quick spurts, often holding tail slightly curved. Frequently stands on hind feet in kangaroo fashion. An excellent climber and is able to jump several inches into the air. Presumably uses its sense of smell to hunt for small insect prey in leaf litter. Also feeds on limited amounts of plant material.

Smoky Shrew
Sorex fumeus

Family: Shrews (Soricidae)

Size: L 2-3" (5-7.5 cm); T 1½-2" (4-5 cm)

Weight: ¼-⅓ oz. (7-9 g)

Description: Light brown above during summer, paler below. Dark gray to nearly black in winter, pale gray below. Narrow, pointed pink snout. Tiny dark eyes. Long tail, not as long as the body, uniform in color. Small pink feet, sometimes with white upper surfaces. Ears barely visible, positioned at the same level as the eyes.

Origin/Age: native; 1-2 years

Compare: Southern Short-tailed Shrew (pg. 57) is larger and has a slightly shorter tail. The Southeastern Shrew (pg. 53) has a bicolored tail that is shorter than that of Smoky Shrew.

Habitat: wet meadows, moist forests, shrubby areas

Home: chamber in an underground burrow, nest made with dried leaves and grasses

Food: insectivore, carnivore; beetles, crickets, spiders, grasshoppers, slugs, earthworms, snails, small mammals

Sounds: inconsequential; sharp squeaks and high-pitched whistles can be heard from up to 2' (61 cm) away

Breeding: Mar-Aug mating; 21-23 days gestation

Young: 2-7 offspring several times per year; born naked with eyes closed, weaned at about 3 weeks

Signs: partially eaten insects near the burrow entrance; extremely tiny, dark scat, widely scattered

Activity: nocturnal, sometimes diurnal; active year-round

Tracks: hind paw ½" (1 cm) long, forepaw ¼" (.6 cm); 1 set of 4 tracks, but prints are so close together they appear to be 1 track; 4 prints together are 1 square inch (6.5 sq. cm)

Stan's Notes: One of the few shrews that has a different color in summer and winter. In Georgia it has a dark dorsal stripe that extends onto its forelimbs, with a pale side.

One of Georgia's uncommon shrews, seen only in the northern third of the state. Range extends from Georgia up into New England and across southern Canada.

Active throughout the year. Known to live in the leaf litter of moist deciduous and coniferous forests. Sometimes found in wetter areas such as bogs and swamps. Populations are often clumped or bunched in suitable habitats or nonexistent.

Hunts on runways above the surface and under the ground in tunnels. Feeds mainly on earthworms, centipedes, sowbugs and insect larvae, but has been known to kill and eat salamanders. Total weight of prey consumed daily equals about half of its own body weight. Like other shrew species, it uses echolocation to find prey in the dark, constantly emitting a sound while hunting.

Young stay in the nest until they reach adult size. Does not breed until 1 year of age, but life expectancy is only 15-17 months.

Southeastern Shrew
Sorex longirostris

Family: Shrews (Soricidae)

Size: L 2-3" (5-7.5 cm); T 1-1¼" (2.5-3 cm)

Weight: ⅟₁₆-⅛ oz. (2-4 g)

Description: Overall reddish brown with a gray belly. A very long, pointed and nearly naked snout. Tiny dark eyes. Ears slightly visible. Short bicolored tail, reddish brown above and lighter below with a short tuft at the tip.

Origin/Age: native; 1-2 years

Compare: The Southern Short-tailed Shrew (pg. 57) and Northern Short-tailed Shrew (pg. 61) are larger and darker in color overall. Least Shrew (pg. 37) is slightly smaller and has a shorter tail.

Habitat: wet meadows, pine forests, plantations, fields, wetlands, moist deciduous forests

Home: nest, 4-6" (10-15 cm) wide, made of leaves and grasses, under a log or rock, near wetlands

Food: insectivore, carnivore; insects, ants, slugs, spiders, earthworms, small mammals such as mice

Sounds: inconsequential; sharp squeaks and high-pitched whistles, gives a series of clicks and twitters

Breeding: spring to autumn mating; 18 days gestation

Young: 2-6 offspring 2-3 times per year; young are born naked with eyes closed, eyes open at 17-19 days, weaned at about 20 days, on their own within days of being weaned

Signs: tiny 170, 172 or runways in freshly dug soil; shrew is rarely, if ever, seen

Activity: diurnal, nocturnal; active year-round

Tracks: hind paw ½" (1 cm) long, forepaw slightly smaller; 1 set of 4 tracks, but prints are so close together they look like 1 track; 4 prints together are 1 square inch (6.5 sq. cm), sometimes has a slight tail drag mark

Stan's Notes: This secretive, solitary animal is rarely seen due to its underground lifestyle. Range extends from southern Illinois and Missouri east to the Maryland coast and south throughout Georgia into central Florida. One of the most common shrews in Georgia.

Not a well-studied mammal, but a good species to have around because it eats many insects and spiders. A discrete animal that does not pose problems for people. Due to the damp nature of soils in Georgia, there are not a lot of digging animals such as shrews. Consequently, shrews are often found in woodpiles and under old wooden buildings that have fallen down. Tunnels are just below the ground or on the surface.

Shrews have poor vision and hold their eyes shut tightly when burrowing underground. They communicate with each other by a series of clicks and twitters and also through echolocation, a type of communication that is not well understood.

Shrews are fierce predators, but they are also near the bottom of the food chain. They are eaten by many larger predators, from bobcats to coyotes to a whole host of avian predators such as owls, hawks and eagles.

Also called Bachman's Shrew in honor of naturalist John Bachman, who discovered the species in 1837. The genus *Sorex* is Latin for "shrew" or "mouse." The species *longirostris* is from the Latin word *longus*, meaning "long" and "rostrum," referring to its snout. Taken together, it is a shrew with a long snout, which best describes the long, nearly naked snout.

Southern Short-tailed Shrew
Blarina carolinensis

Family: Shrews (Soricidae)

Size: L 3-4" (7.5-10 cm); T ¾-1" (2-2.5 cm)

Weight: ⅛-¾ oz. (4-21 g)

Description: Overall dark to slate gray, with a short, nearly naked tail. Long pointed snout. Small pink feet. Tiny dark eyes, usually not noticed. Ears barely visible. Younger individuals are often darker.

Origin/Age: native; 1-2 years

Compare: Northern Short-tailed Shrew (pg. 61) is similar and difficult to tell apart. Use the range maps to help identify. Least Shrew (pg. 37) is smaller and grayer. Southeastern Shrew (pg. 53) is smaller and has a shorter naked snout and longer tail.

Habitat: wide variety of habitats such as moist deciduous woodlands, coniferous forests, fields, meadows, yards and gardens

Home: bulky nest, 6-10" (15-25 cm) wide, made from dried grasses and leaves, usually beneath a log or rock or inside a rotting stump

Food: insectivore; beetles, earthworms, snails, spiders, mice, voles, toads, subterranean fungi

Sounds: inconsequential; sharp squeaks and high-pitched whistles can be heard up to 10' (3 m) away

Breeding: Mar-Jun and Sep-Nov mating; 21-22 days gestation

Young: 2-6 offspring twice per year; born only as large as a honeybee, naked with eyes closed, with adult teeth and can chew, weaned after about 2 days

57

Signs: well-worn inch-wide runways or tunnels through grass or sand, piles of snail shells and insect parts under a log, fallen tree bark or other shelter

Activity: diurnal, nocturnal; active year-round

Tracks: hind paw ⅜-½" (.9-1 cm) long, forepaw slightly smaller; continuous grooves in sand or runways in lawns with no distinct prints; continuous grooves and runways are due to its low-slung body and short legs, which do not allow it to hop or jump

Stan's Notes: One of eight shrew species in Georgia, occurring mostly in the southern half of the state. Although widespread, shrews in Georgia are hard to find and observe. Populations can increase to very high and then drop suddenly, making these small mammals more abundant one year and absent the next.

Slightly smaller, but very similar to its northern cousin, Northern Short-tailed Shrew (pg. 61); range maps will help identify. Most of what is known about the Southern Short-tailed comes from observations of the Northern.

Unique because the Southern and Northern Short-tailed Shrews are the only North American mammals that produce a poisonous saliva. Cannot inject the poison, but chews it into a wound. The poison paralyzes small prey such as mice; can cause tingling and numbness in people.

A solitary shrew. Excavates tunnels underground or runways just below leaf litter, where it patrols for food. Ears and eyes function, but usually go unnoticed because they are so small. Finds most of its prey by smell and feel. Uses ultrasonic clicks (echolocation) to detect objects in dark tunnels, much like a bat. Hunts for short periods of 3-5 minutes, then rests for 20-30 minutes. Consumes half its own weight in food every day. Caches food underground, returning often to eat and replenish the supply. Many cannot live more than 24-48 hours in captivity without food and water. They have a heart rate of one thousand beats per minute.

The male will scent mark its territory with urine, feces or oily secretions from glands near the base of the tail. Marking territory helps reduce the chance of a fatal encounter since rival neighbors will sometimes fight each other to death. Scent marking also advertises social status, helps to attract mates and, as an added benefit, may deter predators that find the glands distasteful.

The female is ready to reproduce as early as 46 days. Mates may stay together for long periods, maybe even for life.

Northern Short-tailed Shrew
Blarina brevicauda

Family: Shrews (Soricidae)

Size: L 3-4" (7.5-10 cm); T ¾-1" (2-2.5 cm)

Weight: ½-1 oz. (14-28 g)

Description: Overall dark to slate gray (younger shrews often darker). Long pointed snout. Small pink feet. Short, nearly naked tail. Tiny dark eyes, often not noticed. Ears barely visible.

Origin/Age: native; 1-2 years

Compare: Southern Short-tailed Shrew (pg. 57) is slightly smaller, but otherwise identical. Masked Shrew (pg. 41) is much smaller, has a longer, narrower snout and longer tail. Least Shrew (pg. 37) is smaller, grayer and found throughout Georgia. Pygmy Shrew (pg. 45) is smaller, light brown and has a longer tail.

Habitat: wide variety; moist deciduous woodlands, fields, coniferous forests, meadows, yards, gardens

Home: bulky nest, 6-10" (15-25 cm) wide, made from dried grasses and leaves, usually beneath a log or rock or inside a rotting stump

Food: insectivore, carnivore; beetles, earthworms, snails, spiders, mice, voles, toads, subterranean fungi

Sounds: inconsequential; sharp squeaks and high-pitched whistles can be heard from a distance of up to 10' (3 m) or more

Breeding: Apr-Aug mating; 21-22 days gestation

Young: 4-7 offspring once per year; born only as large as a honeybee and naked with eyes closed, weaned after about 2 days

Signs: well-worn inch-wide runways or tunnels through grass or snow, partially eaten mice and toads, piles of snail shells and insect parts under a log, fallen tree bark or other shelter

Activity: diurnal, nocturnal; active year-round

Tracks: hind paw ½-¾" (1-2 cm) long, forepaw slightly smaller; continuous grooves in snow or runways in lawns with no distinct prints; continuous grooves and runways are due to its low-slung body and short legs, which do not allow it to hop or jump

Stan's Notes: One of the largest shrews in the state. Northern Short-tailed populations vary, climbing to very high levels and then dropping suddenly, making it seem like it is everywhere one year and nonexistent the next.

A unique species because it is the only North American mammal besides the Southern Short-tailed Shrew (pg. 57) that produces a poisonous saliva. It cannot inject the poison, but chews it into a wound. The poison paralyzes small prey such as mice; can cause tingling and numbness in people.

A solitary shrew. Excavates tunnels underground or runways just below leaf litter, where it patrols for food. Ears and eyes function, but usually go unnoticed because they are so small. Finds most of its prey by smell and feel. Uses ultrasonic clicks (echolocation) to detect objects in dark tunnels, much like a bat. Hunts for short periods of 3-5 minutes, then rests for 20-30 minutes. Consumes half its own weight in food every day. Caches food underground, returning often to eat and replenish the supply.

Many cannot live more than 48 hours in captivity without food and water. Its large size enables this shrew to conserve heat and live longer without food than the other shrews. Smaller shrews cannot live more than 24 hours without food and water.

The male will scent mark its territory with urine, feces or oily secretions from glands near the base of the tail. Marking territory helps reduce the chance of a fatal encounter since rival neighbors will sometimes fight each other to death. Scent marking also advertises social status, helps to attract mates and, as an added benefit, may deter predators that find the glands distasteful.

The female is ready to reproduce as early as 46 days. Mates may stay together for long periods, maybe even for life.

Water Shrew
Sorex palustris

Family: Shrews (Soricidae)

Size: L 4-5" (10-13 cm); T 2-3" (5-7.5 cm)

Weight: ½ oz. (14 g)

Description: Overall dark brown to black with a bright white belly. Long pointed snout. Tiny dark eyes. Fringe of stiff hairs on back of feet. Very long tail, nearly half its total length. Ears not visible.

Origin/Age: native; 3-5 years

Compare: Long pointed snout like the other shrews, but its extremely long tail and the aquatic lifestyle make it easy to differentiate. The distinctive black body and white belly also help to identify.

Habitat: lakes, bogs, streams, ponds

Home: bulky nest, 6-10" (15-25 cm) wide, made with dried grasses and leaves, usually in or near a sphagnum bog mound, beneath a fallen log or inside a rotting stump

Food: insectivore, carnivore; aquatic insects, spiders, slugs, earthworms, leeches, small fish

Sounds: inconsequential; sharp squeaks and high-pitched whistles

Breeding: Jan-Aug mating; 21 days gestation

Young: 5-8 offspring up to 3 times per year; born naked with eyes closed, young do not enter water until they are fully furred

Signs: splashing at the edge of water during the night, small runways in moss along the banks of lakes and streams

Activity: nocturnal, diurnal; most active after dark (especially in summer), usually not seen in the winter

Tracks: hind paw ¼-½" (.6-1 cm) long, forepaw slightly smaller; 1 set of 4 tracks, but prints are so close together they appear as 1 track; 4 prints together are 1 square inch (6.5 sq. cm), has a tail drag mark leading in or out of open water or in snow, lacking a tail drag mark in mud during warm weather

Stan's Notes: One of the least common shrews in Georgia. As the name implies, it lives near or in the water and is found in the far northeastern edge of the state.

This shrew can actually run across the surface of calm water, thanks to the fringe of hairs on its hind feet, which trap oxygen and increase the surface area. Splashing sounds made while it runs can often be heard at night, but the animal moves so quickly it is hard to spot with a flashlight. The hairs also act like fins, aiding underwater swimming. The shrew uses these hairs like a comb to help remove water from its velvety fur, which is water resistant and dries very quickly.

Air trapped in the fur helps the Water Shrew to surface rapidly after diving to the bottom of lakes, streams or bogs or, when it stops swimming, to pop to the surface like a cork.

fringe of hairs

The female may not reproduce until her second year. A mother Water Shrew has only six teats. If she has more than six young, those unable to nurse will most certainly die due to their nearly constant need to feed.

Star-nosed Mole
Condylura cristata

Family: Moles (Talpidae)

Size: L 3-7" (7.5-18 cm); T ¾-1¼" (2-3 cm)

Weight: 1-2½ oz. (28-71 g)

Description: Fur is dark gray to nearly black. Twenty or more thin, fleshy pink projections on nose in a circular pattern. Short legs. Extremely large front feet with long, well-defined claws. A long tail with sparse hair, constricted at the base. Invisible ears. Pinpoint eyes, often hidden.

Origin/Age: native; 1-2 years

Compare: Spends more of its time above the ground than the Eastern Mole (pg. 73). Look for large, fleshy pink projections on the nose to help identify.

Habitat: wet woodlands, moist fields, wetlands, ponds, lakes, streams

Home: burrow, beneath a log or fallen tree, nest is lined with dead leaves and grasses during summer, in a chamber connected to a tunnel system below the frost line during winter, separate chambers for giving birth and raising young

Food: insectivore, carnivore; insects, slugs, earthworms, crustaceans, fish

Sounds: inconsequential; rarely, if ever, heard

Breeding: Apr-May mating; 35-45 days gestation; starts to breed at 10 months

Young: 3-7 (average 5) offspring once per year in April or May, some born as late as August; born naked, helpless, with the "star" nose enclosed in a thin translucent membrane and eyes closed

69

Signs: ridges as a result of tunneling near the surface of soil, mounds of fresh soil (molehills) pushed up during construction of tunnels, runways on the surface leading to and from holes in the ground

Activity: diurnal, nocturnal; active year-round, spends less time underground than other moles

Tracks: hind paw 1" (2.5 cm) long with 5 toes, forepaw 1½" (4 cm) long with 5 toes; individual tracks are indistinguishable and create a single groove with claw marks, sometimes has a tail drag mark

Stan's Notes: An easily recognizable mole in Georgia, but not very common; occurs only in portions of the state. The fleshy, tentacle-like pink nose and long tail make it easy to identify. Nose projections (nasal rays) are presumably used to feel for worms in the darkness underground. Recent studies have indicated they contain highly sensitive tactile organs called Eimer's organs, believed to detect electrical fields given by prey. It is also thought that nasal rays help a mole manipulate objects such as food during capturing and eating. The tail fattens during spring and summer, presumably as an energy store for the breeding season and coming winter, thickening as a result of fat deposition. Main prey are earthworms and insects.

Eyes are tiny and probably useful only to detect light. Digs less powerfully than the more common Eastern Mole (pg. 73), but is a very good swimmer. Can dive after aquatic animals, including fish. Propels itself underwater by moving its feet and tail for extra propulsion. Also a good tunneler, with tunnels often opening out underwater. Has additional aboveground paths or "runs."

Often gregarious and even colonial. Active under snow and even beneath the ice of frozen lakes and streams. Babies grow quickly, leaving nests and mothers at 3-4 weeks.

The genus name *Condylura* is Greek and means "knobby tail," referring to one of the first and, unfortunately, inaccurate drawings of this animal showing a bumpy or knobby tail, much like a string of beads. The species name *cristata* is Latin for "crest" or "tuft" and refers to the star-shaped pattern of projections on the nose. There are six other mole species north of Mexico in North America.

Eastern Mole

Scalopus aquaticus

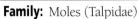

Family: Moles (Talpidae)

Size: L 4-7" (10-18 cm); T ¾-1¼" (2-3 cm)

Weight: 3-5 oz. (85-142 g)

Description: Short silky fur, dark brown to gray with a silver sheen. Long pointed snout. Very large, naked front feet, more wide than long and resembling human hands with palms turned outward. Very short, nearly naked tail. Pinpoint eyes, frequently hidden by fur. Male slightly larger than female.

Origin/Age: native; 1-2 years

Compare: A unique-looking mammal with extremely short legs, no visible eyes, a short tail and large, human-like pink hands for paws. The Star-nosed Mole (pg. 69) has pink projections on its nose. Hairy-tailed Mole (pg. 77) has a hairy tail.

Habitat: dry grassy areas, fields, lawns, gardens, loose well-drained soils

Home: burrow, tunnels usually are 4-20" (10-50 cm) underground in summer, deeper tunnels below the frost line during winter, nest is in a chamber connected to a tunnel, with separate chambers for giving birth and raising young

Food: insectivore, herbivore; insects, grubs, roots, earthworms

Sounds: inconsequential; rarely, if ever, heard

Breeding: Feb-Mar mating; 32-42 days gestation

Young: 2-6 offspring once per year in early spring; born naked with eyes closed, weaned at 30-40 days, leaves nest chamber when weaned

Signs: ridges of soil from tunnel construction just below the surface of the ground, sometimes small piles of soil on the ground (molehills) from digging deeper permanent tunnels

Activity: diurnal, nocturnal; active year-round, does not appear to time its activities with the rising and setting of the sun

Tracks: hind paw ⅝" (1.5 cm) long with 5 toes, forepaw 1½" (4 cm) long with 5 toes; individual tracks are indistinguishable and create a single groove with claw marks, sometimes has a tail drag mark; spends almost all of its time in its underground tunnel system, so tracks are rarely seen

74

Stan's Notes: The first time this animal was described in records was when a drowned mole was found in a well. It was presumed, in error, to be aquatic; hence the Latin species name *aquaticus*, which also refers to the slight webbing between its toes. This is the most subterranean mammal in Georgia, spending 99 percent of its life underground. Also called Common Mole or just Mole.

The Eastern Mole has no external ears. Its tiny eyes are covered with skin and detect light only, not shapes or colors. It has large white teeth, unlike the shrews, which have chestnut or tan teeth. Uses its very sensitive, flexible snout to find food by smelling and sensing vibrations with its whiskers. The nap of its short fur can lie forward or backward, making it easier to travel in either direction in tight tunnels. A narrow pelvis allows it to somersault often and reverse its heading.

Excavates its own tunnel system. Uses its front feet to dig while pushing loosened soil back and out of the way with its hind feet. Able to dig 12 inches (30 cm) per minute in loose soil. Digging and tunneling is beneficial to the environment; it aerates the soil and allows moisture to penetrate deeper into the ground.

Searches for subterranean insects, earthworms, some plant roots and other food in temporary tunnels, usually located just below the surface of the ground. Deeper permanent tunnels are used for living, nesting and depositing waste.

The male will seek out a female in her tunnel to mate during late winter. It is thought that a female rarely leaves her tunnel system except when a young female leaves the tunnels of her mother to establish her own.

Unlike most other small mammals, it reproduces only once each year. Not preyed upon as heavily due to its burrowing (fossorial) life, so does not need to reproduce often.

Hairy-tailed Mole
Parascalops breweri

Family: Moles (Talpidae)

Size: L 5-6" (13-15 cm); T 1-1¼" (2.5-3 cm)

Weight: 1-2 oz. (28-57 g)

Description: Silver gray to nearly black and silvery gray below. Narrow pointed pink (sometimes white) snout. Short legs. Pink-to-white feet. Extremely large front feet with long well-defined claws. Thick hairy tail, black at the base, less than one-quarter the length of the body. Invisible ears. Pinpoint eyes, often hidden. Male is larger than female.

Origin/Age: native; 2-4 years

Compare: Eastern Mole (pg. 73) has a longer snout and less hairy tail than Hairy-tailed. Very uncommon in Georgia. Use range maps to help identify.

Habitat: wide variety of habitats including coniferous and deciduous woodlands, moist fields, roadsides

Home: burrow, underneath a log or fallen tree, nest is lined with dead leaves and grasses in summer, in a chamber connected to a tunnel system that is deeper during winter, with separate chambers for giving birth and raising young

Food: insectivore; beetles, other insects, slugs, worms

Sounds: inconsequential; rarely, if ever, heard

Breeding: Mar-Apr mating; 30-42 days gestation

Young: 4-5 (average 5) offspring once per year in April or May; born naked, helpless, with eyes closed, young are weaned at 4 weeks, sexually mature at 10 months

Signs: ridges as a result of tunneling near the surface of soil, mounds of fresh soil (molehills) pushed up during construction of tunnels, runways on the surface leading to and from holes in the ground

Activity: diurnal, nocturnal; active all year, closer to the surface of the ground during summer, deeper during winter

Tracks: hind paw ¾" (2 cm) long with 5 toes, forepaw 1½" (4 cm) long with 5 toes; individual tracks are indistinguishable and create a single groove with claw marks

Stan's Notes: A large and conspicuous mole with a thick hairy tail, making it fairly easy to identify. Tail is less than one-quarter of the body length. Most have black tails; some have white tips.

Unusual in that the males are noticeably larger than the females (sexually dimorphic). This mole has a total of 44 teeth, making it second only to the opossum for the most teeth in a mammal species in the United States. Very unusual front feet, wider than long, with long claws–perfect for digging in soils. Tunneling can produce a lot of dirt mounds in parks and yards.

It has a small home range of less than ¼ acre (.1 ha). In Georgia, it occurs only in the far northeastern corner of the state, but the range stretches northward into New England as far as central Maine and westward into Canada. Found mainly along the Appalachian Mountains. Tends to live in higher elevations such as the Springer Mountains in Georgia.

Lives alone during non-breeding season in winter. Males leave their burrow system to locate females during spring for mating. After mating, the males return to their burrows while females build nest chambers in the deepest part of the system, lining the cavities with leaves. Mothers with their babies are found in the burrows later in summer.

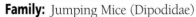

Meadow Jumping Mouse
Zapus hudsonius

Family: Jumping Mice (Dipodidae)

Size: L 2-3" (5-7.5 cm); T 4-6" (10-15 cm)

Weight: ¾-1 oz. (21-28 g)

Description: A reddish brown back with lighter brown sides. May have a dark stripe down the center of back. White belly hair. Large round ears. Prominent dark eyes. Long snout. Extremely long tail, dark above and white below.

Origin/Age: native; 1-2 years

Compare: Smaller overall with a shorter tail than Woodland Jumping Mouse (pg. 97) and lacks the distinctive tricolored body. The Woodland Jumping Mouse is found in coniferous forests in far northeastern Georgia, while Meadow Jumping Mouse is seen in open regions in the upper two-thirds of the state. Other species of mice have belly hair that is gray at the base and tails that are shorter than those of jumping mice.

Habitat: semi-woodlands, moist open fields

Home: nest made from dried grass, under a fallen log or clump of grass; used for hibernation

Food: herbivore, insectivore; underground fungi, seeds, fruit, insects

Sounds: inconsequential; scratching and scampering, drums front feet on ground when threatened

Breeding: May-Jul mating; 17-21 days gestation; will mate shortly after emerging from hibernation

Young: 4-7 pups twice per year; born naked with eyes closed

81

Signs: surface runways leading in many directions, grasses with missing seed heads (topped), piles of grass stems that are the same length and have seed heads removed

Activity: nocturnal; active 5-6 months of the year, hibernating from October to April or May

Tracks: hind paw 1¼" (3 cm) long with a long narrow heel and 5 toes, forepaw ½" (1 cm) long with 4 toes; 1 set of 4 tracks; tracks seen only in mud during months of activity

Stan's Notes: The jumping mouse got its name from its ability to leap up to 3 feet (1 m) to escape predators or when it is startled. Although the name implies that it jumps to get around, it usually walks on all four feet or moves in a series of small jumps.

Often will remain motionless after jumping several times. Uses its long tail, which is more than 50 percent of its total length, for balance while jumping. Hind legs are longer than front legs and are very fragile, often breaking when live-trapped for research.

Feeds during the summer on an underground fungus called *Endogone*, which it finds by smell. Does not store any food for winter, feeding heavily instead during the last month before it hibernates. Will gain up to 100 percent of its body weight in fat. It is a true hibernator, not active in winter. Male emerges from hibernation in April, female a couple weeks later. Some studies show that many apparently do not survive the winter, as only half the population appears the following spring.

Matures sexually before reaching 1 year of age. Many females that were born in springtime are breeding in July. Reproduces twice each year.

This mouse does not cause crop damage and will rarely enter a dwelling. Jumping mice (genera *Zapus* and *Napaeozapus*) are found only in North America.

Eastern Harvest Mouse

Reithrodontomys humulis

Family: Rats and Mice (Muridae)

Size: L 2¼-2¾" (5.5-7 cm); T 2-2¼" (5-5.5 cm)

Weight: ¼-⅜ oz. (7-11 g)

Description: Overall dark brown fur, nearly black down the center of back and reddish brown on the sides. Grayish white underbelly. Large dark ears and large eyes. Tail is thin, nearly naked, somewhat bicolored, not tufted and equal to the length of the head and body combined. Gray or nearly white feet. Grooved front teeth (upper incisors).

Origin/Age: native; 1-2 years

Compare: House Mouse (pg. 93) is larger and overall gray. Unlike the House, Eastern Harvest usually does not enter buildings. Smaller than Golden Mouse (pg. 109), which is overall golden brown.

Habitat: wet grassy areas, fields, roadsides, sedge patches, wetlands

Home: underground burrow with multiple chambers, aboveground ball-shaped nest made of dried grass, 5-6" (13-15 cm) diameter, occasionally low in a shrub or small tree or attached to grass stems, often in an old bird nest

Food: herbivore, insectivore; seeds, vegetation, fruit, fresh green shoots in spring, insects

Sounds: inconsequential; high-pitched trilling call

Breeding: year-round mating; 21-22 days gestation

Young: 3-5 (average 4) pups up to 4 times per year; born naked with eyes closed, weighing about ½ oz. (14 g)

Signs: surface runways, ball-shaped nest made of dried grass on the ground, most obvious after a field or grassland fire, nest is sometimes attached to grass stems or in a small tree or shrub

Activity: mostly nocturnal; active year-round, often huddles in nest during the day with other members of its family

Tracks: hind paw ½" (1 cm) long with 5 toes, forepaw ⅛" (.3 cm) long with 4 toes; sometimes has a tail drag mark

Stan's Notes: The smallest of harvest mice, ranging from Texas east to Georgia, up the East coast to Maryland and across to the southern tip of Illinois. It harvests dried grass to build a large softball-sized nest, hence the common name. Known to use the nest of a bird as a base to build a ball nest of dried grass. Uses underground burrows, but may use more than one nest in its home range, including one or two in shrubs. Uses the runways and burrows of other animals such as pocket gophers and voles.

Considered to be a good mouse to have around because it feeds heavily on weed seeds. Stores many seeds in caches underground. A big climber, jumping into trees and shrubs and scurrying about among the branches. Tolerant of one another and not territorial. Rarely enters homes or other buildings.

A female usually has up to four litters per season. However, it has been reported that a captive female harvest mouse reproduced as many as 14 times, giving birth to a total of 58 young.

The Eastern and other harvest mouse species have been classi-fied in *Reithrodontomys*, a genus separate from other small mice. One way to identify a harvest mouse is by the groove front-and-center in its upper incisor teeth, which other small mice lack. In addition, the harvest mouse lacks the fur-lined cheek pouches of pocket mice. Although some pocket mouse species have grooved incisors like those of harvest mice, this is not a feature that a casual observer will see.

Can be extremely abundant where it occurs, often with very high population densities. Can survive a long time without drinking free-standing water. Presumably obtains all of its water needs through the diet.

Oldfield Mouse
Peromyscus polionotus

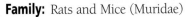

Family: Rats and Mice (Muridae)

Size: L 2½-3" (6-7.5 cm); T 1¾-2" (4.5-5 cm)

Weight: ¼-½ oz. (7-14 g)

Description: Overall tan to light gray with a white chin, chest, belly, legs and feet. Bicolored tail, with the same colors as the body, but sparsely furred, lacking a tuft and much shorter than the length of the head and body. Large, round naked ears.

Origin/Age: native; 6 months to 2 years

Compare: The closer to the coast, the lighter gray the fur. The Cotton Mouse (pg. 113) is larger and darker, with a longer tail. The Eastern Harvest Mouse (pg. 85) is darker, with a gray belly and grooved upper incisors.

Habitat: old fields, vacant farms, beaches, sand dunes, dry scrub

Home: nest in underground tunnels that it excavates, almost always nests in sandy soils to facilitate the extensive burrowing

Food: herbivore, insectivore; seeds, vegetation, fruit, nuts, insects

Sounds: inconsequential

Breeding: year-round mating; 22-24 days gestation

Young: 3-5 pups up to 3-4 times per year; born with eyes and ears closed, opening 13-14 days later

Signs: stockpiles of seeds in underground nest chambers, strong smell of urine in the areas it often visits; small, hard black scat the size of a pinhead

Activity: nocturnal

Tracks: hind paw ¾" (2 cm) long with 5 toes, forepaw ⅝" (1.5 cm) long with 4 toes; 1 set of 4 tracks; sometimes has a tail drag mark

Stan's Notes: A mouse of old fields, abandoned farms and home-steads throughout most of the state. Also in beaches and sand dunes along the coast.

The Oldfield Mouse is by far the lightest colored mouse species in Georgia. The closer to the coast and sandier the habitat, the lighter gray the mouse appears, presumably to blend in better with lighter, sandy environments. Many islands along the Atlantic coast and northern Gulf coast have their own unique subspecies. Some of these subspecies are so light in color that they appear to be almost entirely white.

Highly nocturnal, coming out only at night to feed on seeds and insects. Stores large amounts of seed in its burrow. Most tunnels are only 12-36 inches (30-91 cm) beneath the ground surface. Each tunnel has a main entrance and an escape tunnel. A small amount of sand usually marks the entrance of the main tunnel.

Adult females are slightly larger than adult males. The species is monogamous, with pairs staying together for their entire life. Life span is only 6 months to 2 years. Breeds year-round in Georgia, but mating declines slightly during the summer months. Never leaves its small home territory.

Beneficial to have around because it eats many weed seeds and insects. It is also food for many predator species such as hawks, owls, snakes, foxes and more.

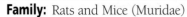

House Mouse
Mus musculus

Family: Rats and Mice (Muridae)

Size: L 2½-4" (6-10 cm); T 2-4" (5-10 cm)

Weight: ½-¾ oz. (14-21 g)

Description: Gray to light brown above, slightly lighter gray below. Large ears. Tail is gray above, naked and nearly the same length as the body.

Origin/Age: non-native; 1-2 years

Compare: Smaller than White-footed Mouse (pg. 101) and Deer Mouse (pg. 105), but House Mouse has a naked tail and is grayer than other mice. Eastern Harvest Mouse (pg. 85) is smaller, overall brown and normally does not enter homes and other buildings. House Mouse is one of the smaller mouse species seen throughout Georgia, making it easy to identify.

Habitat: houses, buildings, cultivated fields

Home: nest with a hollow center, mass of plant or man-made material such as paper or insulation

Food: herbivore, insectivore; seeds, vegetation, fruit, nuts, insects

Sounds: inconsequential; scampering or scratching can be heard

Breeding: Mar-Oct mating; 18-21 days gestation

Young: 2-15 pups 3-4 times per year; born naked with eyes closed

Signs: strong smell of urine in the areas it often visits; small, hard black droppings the size of a pinhead

Activity: nocturnal; active year-round

scat

Tracks: hind paw ½" (1 cm) long with 5 toes, forepaw ¼" (.6 cm) long with 4 toes; 1 set of 4 tracks; sometimes has a tail drag mark

Stan's Notes: One of several non-native mammals in the state. Originally from central Asia, it was inadvertently introduced into North America by Spanish ships that landed in the New World in the sixteenth century.

Uncommon in undisturbed areas and frequently associated with people. Competes effectively with and often displaces native mice and voles, making it an unwanted species. Especially not wanted in homes since it is known to carry disease, damage structures and contaminate food. Must live in a heated dwelling such as a barn or home since it cannot tolerate cold or survive a northern winter. However, it thrives in fields in southern states without the assistance of protective structures.

White mice used in laboratory experiments are bred from albino mice of this species. The species name *musculus* comes from the Sanskrit word *musha*, meaning "thief," and refers to its habit of gathering or "stealing" large quantities of food from homes. Will chew just about anything. It even gnaws holes in wood, giving rise to the stereotypical mouse hole in baseboards that are seen in cartoons.

Lives in small to large groups and tolerates overpopulation well. Shares nests, burrows and tunnels with others of its species and performs mutual grooming. While other mouse species become carnivorous when there is overcrowding, a female House Mouse will simply reproduce less often or part of the group will migrate to a new location.

Woodland Jumping Mouse
Napaeozapus insignis

Family: Jumping Mice (Dipodidae)

Size: L 3-4" (7.5-10 cm); T 4-7" (10-18 cm)

Weight: ¾-1 oz. (21-28 g)

Description: A distinctly tricolored body. Back is brown, sides are orange or yellow to light brown and belly is white. Large round ears. Prominent dark eyes. A long snout. Extremely long tail, dark above and white below, usually with a white tip.

Origin/Age: native; 1-2 years

Compare: Jumping mice have longer tails than the other mouse species. Similar to the Meadow Jumping Mouse (pg. 81), which is less distinctly tricolored and lacks a white-tipped tail (tail isn't a reliable field mark). Consider range: Meadow is more widespread, while Woodland is found only in a small area of northern Georgia.

Habitat: coniferous woodlands with much undergrowth, forest edges

Home: nest made of dried grass, under a clump of grass or fallen log; used for hibernation

Food: herbivore, insectivore; fungi, seeds, fruit, insects

Sounds: inconsequential; scratching or scampering can be heard, drums front feet on ground if threatened

Breeding: May-Jun mating; 23-29 days gestation; will mate shortly after emerging from hibernation

Young: 4-7 pups once per year; born naked with eyes closed, eyes open at 26 days, weaned at 1 month

97

Signs: surface runways leading in many directions, grasses with missing seed heads (topped), piles of grass stems that are the same length and have seed heads removed

Activity: nocturnal; active 5-6 months of the year, hibernating from October to April or May

Tracks: hind paw 1¼" (3 cm) long with a long narrow heel and 5 toes, forepaw ½" (1 cm) long with 4 toes; 1 set of 4 tracks; tracks seen only in mud during months of activity

Stan's Notes: One might conclude from its common name that this mouse jumps to get around. Actually, it usually walks on all four feet or moves in a series of small jumps. The common name comes from its ability to leap up to 4 feet (1.2 m) when startled or to escape predators. Jumps several times, then will often stay perfectly still to blend into the environment.

The only member of the genus *Napaeozapus*, this mouse rarely leaves the forest. A full one-third of its diet consists of fungi, with seeds and insects comprising the rest. Feeding on fungi provides the mouse with much needed water. The mouse deposits fungi spores through its excrement, which benefits the fungi.

Like Meadow Jumping Mouse (pg. 81), Woodland is a hibernator, gaining up to 100 percent of its body weight in fat each fall. It is a true hibernator, not active until springtime, with most entering hibernation in October. Males emerge in April, females in May. Apparently many do not survive winter. Some studies indicate only half the population emerges the next spring.

Reproduces only once each year, while Meadow Jumping Mouse reproduces twice. Its gestation period of up to about 4 weeks is much longer than the gestation of the Meadow Jumping Mouse, which is usually only 17-21 days. Gives birth to 4-7 young despite having only four teats, unlike Meadow Jumping Mouse, which has eight.

White-footed Mouse
Peromyscus leucopus

Family: Rats and Mice (Muridae)

Size: L 3-4¼" (7.5-10.5 cm); T 2-3½" (5-9 cm)

Weight: ⅜-1¼ oz. (11-35 g)

Description: Reddish brown back and sides with white chest, belly, legs and feet. Tail is brown above, white below and shorter than the head and body. Large bulging eyes. Large, round naked ears.

Origin/Age: native; 1-2 years

Compare: Hard to distinguish from Deer Mouse (pg. 105). White-footed Mouse is usually slightly smaller, with smaller ears and a slightly shorter tail.

Habitat: wide variety such as woodlands, fields, around dwellings, river bottoms

Home: nest, loose round mass of plant material with a hollow center, lined with animal hair, milkweed silk or other soft material, usually underneath a log or other shelter or inside a log or standing tree; abandons nest when completely soiled with urine and builds another

Food: omnivore; seeds, vegetation, fruit, nuts, insects, baby birds, carrion

Sounds: inconsequential; scratching or scampering can be heard, drums front feet on ground if threatened

Breeding: year-round, but mainly Mar-Oct mating; 22-23 days gestation

Young: 4-6 pups up to 3-4 times per year; born with eyes and ears closed, all gray when very young, dull brown after 40-50 days, reddish brown in a couple months

101

Signs: stockpiles of seeds near nest, strong smell of urine in the areas it often visits; small, hard black scat the size of a pinhead

Activity: nocturnal in summer, more diurnal in winter; remains in the nest during the coldest winter days

Tracks: hind paw ¾" (2 cm) long with 5 toes, forepaw ¼" (.6 cm) long with 4 toes; 1 set of 4 tracks; sometimes has a tail drag mark

Stan's Notes: A common small mammal, occurring in a variety of habitats. Generally more territorial and aggressive than the mild-mannered Deer Mouse (pg. 105). Will bite if handled. Like other mice, it is an important part of the ecosystem, being prey for many animals such as foxes, coyotes, hawks, owls and more.

The range extends from the East coast to Montana and down through Texas to southern Mexico. The White-footed is a great swimmer that has dispersed to islands in the largest lakes.

An excellent climber, often climbing trees to find seeds. Uses its tail to help maintain balance when climbing. Enjoys a variety of food, but eats mainly seeds. Caches food in fall, often nearby in an empty bird nest. Some caches contain over a quart of seeds from a variety of plants. Enters homes in fall for shelter and food.

pup

In the coldest winter months it enters a condition resembling hibernation (torpor), in which body temperature drops and rate of breathing slows from 700 breaths per minute to as few as 60.

Young leave the nest after only 2 weeks and start to breed at about 40 days. They rarely live more than a year, with entirely new populations produced annually. A carrier (vector) for ticks that carry Lyme disease. Use care when cleaning out old mouse nests. Avoid breathing in any airborne dust or particles when removing old nests.

Deer Mouse
Peromyscus maniculatus

Family: Rats and Mice (Muridae)

Size: L 3-4½" (7.5-11 cm); T 2-4" (5-10 cm)

Weight: ⅜-1¼ oz. (11-35 g)

Description: Back and sides highly variable in color from gray to reddish brown. Chest, belly, legs and feet are always white. Tail sharply bicolored, dark above and white below, equal to or shorter than head and body length, with a tufted tip. Large bulging eyes. Large round ears.

Origin/Age: native; 1-2 years

Compare: Very similar to White-footed Mouse (pg. 101), with a slightly longer tail. It is extremely difficult to differentiate these two species because of their remarkable similarities. Use range maps to help identify the Deer Mouse.

Habitat: nearly all habitats including woodlands, prairies, fields, wetlands, scrublands, mountains, around dwellings

Home: nest made of dried plant material and moss, in a small depression in the ground or in an above-ground cavity

Food: omnivore; seeds, vegetation, fruit, nuts, insects, earthworms, baby birds, baby mice, carrion

Sounds: inconsequential; scratching and scampering, drums front feet on ground when threatened

Breeding: Mar-Oct mating; 21-25 days gestation

Young: 1-8 (average 5) pups up to 3 times per year; born naked and deaf with eyes closed, juvenile is gray with a white belly, leaves mother at 3 weeks

Signs: strong smell of urine in the areas it often visits, including its large nest made from dried plant material; small, hard black droppings the size of a pinhead

Activity: nocturnal, crepuscular; active year-round, stays in nest during the coldest winter days or during heavy rain in summer

Tracks: hind paw ¾" (2 cm) long with 5 toes, forepaw ¼" (.6 cm) long with 4 toes; 1 set of 4 tracks; sometimes has a tail drag mark

Stan's Notes: The most widespread rodent in North America, seen in parts of the northern third of Georgia. Found in nearly every habitat from the snowy Arctic Circle to the rain forests in Central America. More than 100 subspecies have been described; differences are in the tail length and ear size. Deer Mouse appears different around the world (morphologically variable), more so than other mouse species.

An important food source for other animals such as foxes, hawks, coyotes and owls. Lives mostly on the ground. Tunnels beneath leaf litter to the surface of the ground and also runs around on top of the ground. May have several emergency escape tunnels in addition to the tunnel that leads to its nest.

Very tame and not aggressive. Climbs trees and shrubs to reach seeds and leaves. Caches food for winter, storing seeds and small nuts in protected areas outside the nest.

Constructs nest during late fall or early winter in a bluebird nest box or another birdhouse. Frequently solitary, but will gather in small groups in winter, usually females with young, to huddle and conserve heat. However, their combined urine quickly soaks the nesting material, necessitating a move to another nest box or natural cavity. Readily enters homes looking for shelter and food.

Sexually mature at 5-7 weeks. Male may stay with female briefly after mating, but frequently lives a solitary life. Female is more territorial than the male, but male has a larger home range. Home territory ranges from a few hundred square feet to a couple acres.

A primary host for the virulent hantavirus that causes Hantaviral Pulmonary Syndrome (HPS), a serious disease in people. Great care must be taken not to breathe in dust or other debris when cleaning out a Deer Mouse nest from a birdhouse or your home.

Golden Mouse
Ochrotomys nuttalli

Family: Rats and Mice (Muridae)

Size: L 3½-4" (9-10 cm); T 3-3½" (7.5-9 cm)

Weight: ¾-1 oz. (21-28 g)

Description: Golden brown back, sometimes tinged yellow on the sides. Creamy white chin and belly. Bicolored tail, matching the color of the body and the same length as the head and body. Tail sparsely haired and semiprehensile. Large, round naked ears.

Origin/Age: native; 1-2 years

Compare: Eastern Harvest Mouse (pg. 85) is much darker and has a shorter tail. Slightly smaller than the Cotton Mouse (pg. 113), which is dark brown to almost black. Golden has a unique color and is one of the easiest mice to identify by this alone.

Habitat: trees, dense tangles of shrubs, oak woods, forests

Home: nest, loose round mass of plant material (such as Spanish moss) with a hollow center, lined with animal hair, milkweed silk or other soft material, 3-30' (.9-9.1 m) above the ground in thick vegetation or Spanish moss, sometimes on the ground; leaves nest when it is soaked with urine

Food: herbivore; seeds, fruit, nuts; also some insects

Sounds: inconsequential; scratching or scampering

Breeding: year-round mating; 22-23 days gestation

Young: 2-5 pups up to 3-4 or more times per year; reddish brown, born with eyes and ears closed, opening 11-14 days later, weaned at 3 weeks, sexually mature at 1-2 months

Signs: globular nests in trees, especially in Spanish moss, some nests are made of pine needles, located in thick tangles of vines, briers or shrubs, sometimes a round nest is constructed in an old bird nest

Activity: nocturnal

Tracks: hind paw ¾" (2 cm) long with 5 toes, forepaw ½" (1 cm) long with 4 toes; 1 set of 4 tracks; spends much of its time in trees (semiarboreal), making tracks uncommon

Stan's Notes: A unique-looking mouse and one of the easiest to identify simply by its color. Also unique because it climbs trees (semiarboreal) and builds its nest off the ground.

A common mouse of southeastern states. Ranges from southern Illinois to Louisiana, east to central Florida and up through Georgia to coastal Virginia. Prefers dense woodlands with abundant cover. Climbs trees, scampering across tree branches, using its tail for balance. Some report that the tail tip is used to help grip (semiprehensile).

Nests mainly in trees, building large ball-shaped nests of plant material such as Spanish moss, pine needles and such. Lines the nest with soft plant material or animal fur. Builds several nests within easy scampering distance. Most are above the surface of the ground; some are on the ground. Has been known to use an old bird nest as a base to make its own nesting chamber. Males and females share the nest until the young are born. After their birth, males no longer enters the nest.

Eats mainly seeds, collecting fruit and seeds from many kinds of plants such as sumac, greenbrier, cherry and even poison ivy. It has specialized internal cheek pouches in which it carries seeds back to feeding platforms in the tree. These are usually areas with flattened vegetation where the mouse will sit and eat what it gathered in the safety of the thick vegetation on the ground.

In other parts of the country, this mouse breeds seasonally. It is a year-round breeder in Georgia, with females giving birth many times each year.

Cotton Mouse
Peromyscus gossypinus

Family: Rats and Mice (Muridae)

Size: L 3¾-4¼" (9.5-10.5 cm); T 3-3½" (7.5-9 cm)

Weight: ¾-1½ oz. (21-43 g)

Description: Overall reddish brown, nearly black on center of back, gradually browner on sides. White chest, belly, legs and feet. Bicolored tail, dark brown above, white below, shorter than head and body. Large bulging eyes. Large, round naked ears. Each hind foot has 6 pads (tubercles) on the sole.

Origin/Age: native; 6 months to 1 year

Compare: Oldfield Mouse (pg. 89) is overall gray, with a short tail. Larger than the House Mouse (pg. 93), which is lighter and lacks a dark center of back.

Habitat: wide variety such as woodlands, fields, swamps, river bottoms, sand dunes, buildings

Home: nest, loose round mass of plant material with a hollow center, lined with cotton, animal hair, milkweed silk or other soft material, under a log or other shelter such as a tortoise burrow, sometimes inside a log or standing tree; abandons nest when soiled with urine and builds another

Food: omnivore; seeds, vegetation, fruit, nuts, insects

Sounds: inconsequential; scratching or scampering can be heard, high-pitched squeak if around other mice

Breeding: year-round, but mainly Mar-Oct mating; 22-23 days gestation

Young: 4-7 pups up to 3-4 times per year; all gray when very young, dull brown after 40-50 days, reddish brown in a couple months

Signs: stockpiles of seeds near nest, strong smell of urine in the areas it often visits; small, hard black scat the size of a pinhead

Activity: nocturnal

Tracks: hind paw 1" (2.5 cm) long with 5 toes, forepaw ¾" (2 cm) long with 4 toes; 1 set of 4 tracks; sometimes has a tail drag mark

Stan's Notes: One of the most common small mammals in the state. Range extends from Florida up through Georgia and the eastern coast to Virginia, west to the southern tip of Illinois and southwest to mid-Texas. Seen in a wide variety of habitats across most of Georgia.

Very closely related to White-footed Mouse (pg. 101) and Deer Mouse (pg. 105). Like other mice, Cotton Mouse is an important part of the ecosystem, serving as prey for many animals such as foxes, coyotes, hawks and owls. It also helps move seeds around, which sprout later and grow.

It is a great swimmer and also an excellent climber, frequently climbing trees to find seeds. Uses its tail to help maintain balance when climbing. Enjoys a variety of food, about 50 percent seed and 50 percent animal and insect.

The species name *gossypinus* originates from the Latin and means "cotton." Does not live in cotton fields, as the common name suggests. Instead, it gathers cotton to line its nest. Builds its nest from plant material beneath downed logs, inside underground burrows or in brush piles. Sometimes builds nest aboveground in trees and shrubs. In fall, enters homes for shelter and food, but not as much as House Mouse (pg. 93) and Norway Rat (pg. 129).

This mouse has six bumps, called tubercles, on the sole of each rear foot. Noting the number of tubercles is a good way to help identify it.

Marsh Rice Rat
Oryzomys palustris

Family: Rats and Mice (Muridae)

Size: L 4½-5½" (11-14 cm); T 4-4½" (10-11 cm)

Weight: 1½-2½ oz. (43-71 g)

Description: Brown with grayish sides and off-white to gray below. Short wide snout. Small round ears. Dark eyes. Tail is scaly and not as long as the length of the body and head combined.

Origin/Age: native; 1-2 years

Compare: Much smaller than Black Rat (pg. 121), which has a naked tail longer than its head and body. Smaller than Hispid Cotton Rat (pg. 125), which appears more grizzled, has a stockier body and darker feet.

Habitat: usually associated with marshes, wetlands, fresh water, saltwater and flooded fields

Home: shallow burrow above high water levels or round nests made of dried grasses, sedges or other plants, usually under logs and other debris above high water, occasionally uses an old bird nest

Food: omnivore; plants, rice, seeds, nuts, insects, birds, bird eggs, small mammals, carrion, snails, crabs

Sounds: usually silent; makes inconsequential noises

Breeding: year-round mating; 20-25 days gestation; female can mate within hours of giving birth

Young: 2-4 (average 3) offspring up to 6 times per year; born naked with eyes closed, eyes open at about 5-6 days, weaned at 2 weeks

Signs: water trails along the surface at the water's edge, cut plants, cut plants on feeding platforms in shallow water

Activity: nocturnal; active year-round, can be active on cloudy days

Tracks: hind paw 1" (2.5 cm) long with a narrow heel and 5 toes, forepaw ½" (1 cm) long with 4 well-spread toes; often follows the same paths over and over, making individual tracks difficult to distinguish

Stan's Notes: This is a small, semiaquatic native rat with a good disposition and habits. Not usually aggressive and does not enter homes or barns, staying mainly in wetlands where it feeds on green plants. Strictly nocturnal.

Occurs from the eastern edge of Texas to Florida and throughout Georgia, up the coast to Maryland and west to the southern tip of Illinois. More common toward the coast and is rarely found away from water such as ponds, streams and lakes. Can be found in wet forest.

Swims underwater, searching for the tender parts of underwater plants. Also eats aquatic insects, snails and tiny crabs. Consumes equal amounts of plant and animal matter, the diet changing with the season and the season's abundance of food. Apparently has an affinity for cultivated rice, which accounts for its common name.

This animal is so small and occurs in such low density, it usually never causes damage to crops or wetland plants and therefore goes unnoticed. Constructs feeding platforms in wetlands with woven grasses and other vegetation. Will bring food back to the platform to eat.

Black Rat
Rattus rattus

Family: Rats and Mice (Muridae)

Size: L 6¼-7½" (15.5-19 cm); T 7-10" (18-25 cm)

Weight: 7-12 oz. (198-340 g)

Description: Dark brown to nearly black above. Only slightly lighter below. Long narrow snout. Large round naked ears. Dark eyes. Very long, scaly tail, longer than the head and body length.

Origin/Age: non-native; 2-4 years

Compare: Hispid Cotton Rat (pg. 125) is slightly larger and looks more grizzled. Eastern Woodrat (pg. 133) has a well-furred tail. The Norway Rat (pg. 129) is brown and has a long naked tail that is shorter than its head and body length; this is unlike the Black Rat, which has a longer tail than its head and body combined.

Habitat: cities, dumps, farms, abandoned buildings, homes

Home: network of tunnels, 2-3" (5-7.5 cm) wide and up to 6' (1.8 m) long, with inner chambers for sleeping and feeding, often has several escape exits and dead-end tunnels for hiding

Food: omnivore; seeds, nuts, insects, carrion, birds, bird eggs, small mammals

Sounds: high-pitched squeaks if squabbling with other rats; scratching, gnawing or scampering at night

Breeding: year-round mating; 21-26 days gestation; female can mate within hours of giving birth

Young: 2-8 (average 5) offspring up to 10 times per year; born naked with eyes closed, eyes open at about 2 weeks, weaned at 3-4 weeks

121

Signs: holes chewed in barn walls or doors, well-worn paths along walls or that lead in and out of chewed holes, smell of urine near the nest site; large, hard, cylindrical, dark brown-to-black droppings deposited along trails

Activity: nocturnal; active year-round, can be active on cloudy days

Tracks: hind paw 1⅜" (3.5 cm) long with a narrow heel and 5 toes, forepaw 1" (2.5 cm) long with 4 well-spread toes; often follows the same paths over and over, making individual tracks difficult to distinguish

Stan's Notes: The Black Rat, a non-native mammal from Asia, is the infamous species that carried bubonic plague. It is by far the most abundant of introduced rats in the state. Common in both rural and urban areas of Georgia, on farms and ranches, as well as in back alleys of the largest cities. A climber, found in barn rafters and running on power lines. Also called House Rat and Roof Rat because it is often seen in homes and on rooftops. Known as Ship Rat since it was found on large sailing ships.

Often makes its nest in the thatch of palm trees. Seen scampering up and down palm tree trunks at night. Comes out at night to feed on palm fruit and can be heard moving about in the trees.

There are many subspecies of Black Rat. Only a few of these are actually black, making it hard to differentiate from Norway Rat (pg. 129). One way to tell them apart is to note the tail length. Black Rat has a longer tail than the length of its head and body combined; Norway Rat has a shorter tail.

Believed to have been first introduced to America in 1609 by the early settlers at Jamestown. It has since spread across the country on its own. Was once much more common in the United States. With the introduction of the Norway Rat, Black Rat numbers have declined.

Hispid Cotton Rat
Sigmodon hispidus

Family: Rats and Mice (Muridae)

Size: L 6-8½" (15-21.5 cm); T 4-5" (10-13 cm)

Weight: 3-5 oz. (85-142 g)

Description: Large-bodied rat. Dark grizzled back and rump, lighter sides and a grayish white belly. Cream eye-ring and small dark eyes. Round ears. Short stout snout. Dark feet. Tail is dark gray above, sparsely haired and slightly shorter than head and body.

Origin/Age: native; 1-4 years

Compare: Marsh Rice Rat (pg. 117) is smaller, leaner and does not appear as grizzled. Hispid Cotton Rat is smaller and more grizzled than the Norway Rat (pg. 129). Black Rat (pg. 121) has a tail longer than its head and body.

Habitat: wide variety from scrublands to grasslands, often near water or wet areas

Home: network of tunnels, 2-3" (5-7.5 cm) wide and up to 6' (1.8 m) long, leading to inner chambers used for sleeping and feeding, often has several escape exits and dead-end tunnels for hiding

Food: herbivore; leaves, seeds, nuts

Sounds: inconsequential; high-pitched squeaks, squeals

Breeding: year-round mating; 25-27 days gestation; female can mate within hours of giving birth

Young: 2-12 (average 6) offspring up to 5 times per year; born well furred and well developed with eyes closed, eyes open at about 60 hours, able to walk and run after birth, weaned at 1-2 weeks

125

Signs: nests made with plant material aboveground and below, well-worn runways in grass

Activity: nocturnal, crepuscular; active year-round, can be active on cloudy days

Tracks: hind paw 1½" (4 cm) long with a narrow heel and 5 toes, forepaw 1" (2.5 cm) long with 4 well-spread toes; often follows the same paths over and over, making individual tracks difficult to distinguish when it has been walking

Stan's Notes: Cotton rats have a stocky body, short round snout, coarse grizzled fur and pleasant disposition. The Hispid is one of the largest of the four cotton rat species in the United States and is the only one that occurs in Georgia.

Cotton rats are active year-round and can be active at any time of day, depending on weather. During rainy years they reproduce much more, with a marked decrease in reproduction during drought years.

Nests are either in chambers underground or aboveground in dense clumps of grass. Similar to harvest mice, the aboveground nests are ball-shaped masses of dried plant material.

Main food is green grass and when available, seeds. This rat will also feed on insects and the eggs of ground-nesting birds.

Marks territories with scents indicating sex, dominance and sexually readiness. Also uses visual signals, such as body postures, to communicate between individuals.

Can breed up to 5 times a year in the wild and up to 10 times a year in captivity. Females often breed shortly after giving birth. Becomes sexually mature in 40 days. Young rats look different from their parents until they reach 6 months. Only the females care for the young.

The common name "Hispid," originating from Latin, refers to its dark, grizzled, stiff hairs and accurately describes the appearance of this tame and timid critter. An important source of food for many predators such as bobcats, coyotes, hawks, eagles, falcons and just about anything that can catch them.

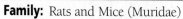

Norway Rat
Rattus norvegicus

Family: Rats and Mice (Muridae)

Size: L 8-10" (20-25 cm); T 5-8" (13-20 cm)

Weight: ½-1 lb. (.2-.5 kg)

Description: Brown to grayish brown above and gray below. Long narrow snout. Large round ears. Dark eyes. Scaly tail, shorter than the body length.

Origin/Age: non-native; 2-4 years

Compare: Larger than all mice, shrews and voles. The Black Rat (pg. 121) has a longer tail than its head and body combined. Eastern Woodrat (pg. 133) has a well-furred tail. Hispid Cotton Rat (pg. 125) is smaller and appears more grizzled. Look for large ears and a long naked tail that is shorter than the head and body length to help identify the Norway Rat.

Habitat: cities, dumps, homes, farms

Home: network of tunnels, 2-3" (5-7.5 cm) wide and up to 6' (1.8 m) long, with inner chambers for sleeping and feeding, often has several escape exits and dead-end tunnels for hiding

Food: omnivore; seeds, nuts, insects, carrion, birds, bird eggs, small mammals

Sounds: high pitched squeaks if squabbling with other rats; scratching, gnawing or scampering at night

Breeding: year-round mating; 20-25 days gestation; female can mate within hours of giving birth

Young: 2-9 (average 6) offspring up to 10 times per year; born naked with eyes closed, eyes open at about 2 weeks, weaned at 3-4 weeks

Signs: holes chewed in barn walls or doors, well-worn paths along walls or that lead in and out of chewed holes, smell of urine near the nest site; large, hard, cylindrical, dark brown-to-black droppings deposited along trails

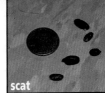
scat

Activity: nocturnal; active year-round, can be active on cloudy days

Tracks: hind paw 1½" (4 cm) long with a narrow heel and 5 toes, forepaw 1" (2.5 cm) long with 4 well-spread toes; often follows the same paths over and over, making individual tracks difficult to distinguish

Stan's Notes: A rat of cities large and small as well as rural areas, including farms. This animal has greatly benefited from its association with people. It has adapted well to city environments, feeding on discarded food and carrion. In farm settings, it eats stored food such as grain.

Also known as Common Rat, Brown Rat, Water Rat or Sewer Rat. A good swimmer and climber. Tolerates cold temperatures well. Excavates by loosening dirt with its front feet, pushes dirt under its belly, then turns and pushes dirt out with its head and front feet. Will chew through roots when they are in the way. A true omnivore, it sometimes acts like a predator, killing chickens and other small farm animals. Can be aggressive if backed into a corner or during a run-in with the family dog. Able to reproduce quickly, especially when food is abundant.

Has a very small territory with a high population density. Will migrate upon occasion. Large numbers have been seen leaving an area, presumably in response to overcrowding and a dwindling food supply.

Despite its common name, the Norway Rat is thought to originate from central Asia. It was introduced to different parts of the world via trading ships in the 1600-1700s and is believed to have been brought to North America in ships that transported grain in the eighteenth century. The name "Norway" actually comes from the fact this species was scientifically described in Norway.

This is the same species as the white rats used in lab experiments. A carrier of disease and fleas and should be exterminated when possible. However, it is difficult to trap and exterminate because its home usually has several escape exits. Due to intense human pressure for eradication (artificial selection), it has now become resistant to many types of rat poisons.

Eastern Woodrat
Neotoma floridana

Family: Rats and Mice (Muridae)

Size: L 7¼-11½" (18.5-29 cm); T 6-7" (15-18 cm)

Weight: 10-16 oz. (284-454 g)

Description: A large mouse-like gray rat. Brown flanks. Gray-to-white (or creamy white) chin, chest and belly. Long pointed snout. Large round ears and large dark eyes. Tail much shorter than body, sharply bicolored, dark above, well furred, lacks a tufted tip. Long black and white whiskers. White feet.

Origin/Age: native; 1-3 years

Compare: The Black Rat (pg. 121) has a very long naked tail and lacks a white chin. Norway Rat (pg. 129) is smaller and has a much shorter tail.

Habitat: wide variety of habitats such as rocky areas, wetlands, scrublands, brushlands and forests

Home: small debris pile or very large nest of many sticks, branches, bones and more (midden), chamber lined with dry vegetation, by a large tree, log or in an abandoned building, with many entrances, can be used by many individual rats over time

Food: herbivore; wide variety of green plants, grasses, fruits, seeds, berries, fungi, very few insects

Sounds: thumping or drumming created by the hind feet, very vocal with much squabbling during flights

Breeding: year-round mating; 25-35 days gestation

Young: 1-5 (average 3) offspring up to 2-3 times per year; born naked with eyes closed, opening at 15 days, weaned at 62-72 days, doesn't become sexually mature until 5-6 months

Signs: large dome-shaped stick house (midden), reminiscent of a brush pile, containing hundreds of sticks, bark, bones and whatever else the animal is able to carry, well-worn trails leading out and away from the midden in many directions, piles of scat outside the midden; pellet-shaped waste

Activity: nocturnal; active year-round, can be active on cloudy days

Tracks: hind paw 1¾" (4.5 cm) long with a narrow heel and 5 toes, forepaw 1¼" (3 cm) long with 4 well-spread toes; frequently follows the same paths over and over, making individual tracks difficult to distinguish when it has been hopping

Stan's Notes: By far the most wide ranging of woodrats. Several species occur in the western half of the country, but this is the only woodrat in the eastern United States. Range extends from central Florida throughout Georgia and up the coast to North Carolina, west to Kansas and south to eastern Texas. Also called Florida Woodrat, which references the species name *floridana*.

Often called Pack Rat due to its habit of collecting sticks, bark, bones and even shiny metal or mineral objects that it stores in and around its den, called a midden. Digs a network of tunnels beneath the midden, especially when there is a limited supply of materials and the midden is small. Builds its nest at the base of a large tree, next to a fallen log or inside an abandoned building.

A solitary animal that is found with others only during mating season and when young are with their mothers. Very aggressive toward one another during the non-breeding season. Fights are common and result in torn ears and damaged tails. Sometimes individuals also have scars on their bodies.

Lodges shed water well, keeping the interior dry and temperate. Does not defecate or urinate in its home, but has a separate toilet outside–evident by piles of pellet-shaped droppings. Normally nocturnal, but sometimes can be seen outside on a cloudy day.

Young are born with front teeth that permit them to grasp their mother's nipple and not let go. If the mother starts walking while nursing, the young will continue to clench and end up getting dragged behind her, bouncing along the ground on their backs.

Southern Red-backed Vole
Clethrionomys gapperi

Family: Rats and Mice (Muridae)

Size: L 3-4" (7.5-10 cm); T 1-2" (2.5-5 cm)

Weight: 1-1½ oz. (28-43 g)

Description: A rusty red back with lighter brown sides. Black belly hair with white tips, making belly appear silvery white. Rounded snout. Small round ears. Small dark eyes. Short tail, bicolored and naked with a small tuft at the tip.

Origin/Age: native; 1-2 years

Compare: Voles have shorter, rounder snouts and shorter tails than mice. Meadow Vole (pg. 145) is larger, has a more grizzled appearance and is not as red. Smaller than Prairie Vole (pg. 149), which is gray brown with no red. Use range to help identify.

Habitat: open wet meadows in coniferous forests, spruce bogs, wetlands, swamps

Home: nest with a hollow center, made of plant material, 3-4" (7.5-10 cm) wide, beneath a log or among tree roots

Food: insectivore, herbivore; insects, green leaves, fruit, seeds, leaf buds, bark of young trees, fungi

Sounds: inconsequential; rarely, if ever, heard

Breeding: late winter to late autumn mating; 17-19 days gestation

Young: 2-8 (average 5) offspring several times per year; born naked, toothless, with eyes closed, body covered with fine hair and eyes open by 12 days, weaned and on its own at about 3 weeks, looks gray until 1-2 months, then turns red

137

Signs: runways in grass leading beneath rocks, cut grass piled up along runways

Activity: diurnal, nocturnal; active year-round, rests and sleeps for several hours, then is active for several hours throughout the day with peaks at dawn and dusk

Tracks: hind paw ¾" (2 cm) long with 5 toes, forepaw slightly smaller with 4 toes; individual tracks are indistinguishable and create a single groove

Stan's Notes: Occurs in a limited habitat in the far northeastern part of Georgia, so not often seen. A short-lived mammal, with most living only 10-12 months; some, however, can survive up to 24 months. Populations peak in fall, with numbers dropping quickly in winter due to predation and starvation. Entire populations of birds of prey may move when vole populations drop.

Active day and night and does not hibernate. Carries on with life underneath snow at high elevations (subnivean), even expanding its home range in that environment. Will follow well-maintained surface trails only occasionally. May use tunnel systems of larger animals. Rarely enters homes or cabins. May store roots, shoots and fungi for later consumption. Underground fungi is an important and much sought food source.

Like all other vole species, the digestive tract of this species has a large pouch called a cecum, which contains microscopic bacteria (microflora). These microflora help to break down items that are hard to digest, such as cellulose, which is the chief component of green plants.

Becomes sexually mature at 5-6 months. The male will stay with the family until the young are weaned. A food staple for weasels, foxes, coyotes and many other mammals. It is also a major food item for many hawk and owl species.

Woodland Vole
Microtus pinetorum

Family: Rats and Mice (Muridae)

Size: L 3¾-4½" (9.5-11 cm); T ½-1¼" (1-3 cm)

Weight: ¾-1¼ oz. (21-35 g)

Description: Overall chestnut brown fur with a glossy or shiny appearance and gray chest and belly. Short blunt snout. Tiny eyes. Small ears, but visible. Short bicolored tail, changing gradually from dark on top to light below.

Origin/Age: native; 1-2 years

Compare: Woodland Vole has a bicolored tail that changes from dark above to light below gradually, unlike the tails of the Meadow Vole (pg. 145) and Prairie Vole (pg. 149), which have sharp color demarcations. Prairie Vole also has a grizzled appearance, with longer, black-tipped fur, which Woodland Vole lacks.

Habitat: deciduous forests with thick leaf litter and green ground cover, dense grass patches

Home: ball-shaped nest with a hollow center, made of dried grasses, usually underground in a network of tunnels; lives mainly below the surface; also maintains a series of surface tunnels

Food: herbivore; green plants in summer; roots, bulbs, seeds, berries and other fruit in winter

Sounds: inconsequential; chatters with up to 5 notes per call when threatened

Breeding: Feb-Oct mating; 20-24 days gestation

Young: 1-4 pups up to 4 times per year; born with eyes and ears closed, weaned at 17 days

Signs: well-worn runways and tunnels through thick vegetation

Activity: nocturnal, diurnal; active year-round, often active 24 hours, with several hours of rest followed by several hours of activity

Tracks: hind paw ⅝" (1.5 cm) long with 5 toes, forepaw ¼" (.6 cm) long with 4 toes; individual tracks are indistinguishable and create a single groove

Stan's Notes: Four vole species (not including the muskrats) are found in Georgia. Woodland Vole occurs throughout most of the state and is much more common than the Prairie Vole (pg. 149) and Southern Red-backed Vole (pg. 137), which are seen only in the northern edge of Georgia. The Meadow Vole (pg. 145) occurs only in the northern half of the state.

A vole of deciduous forests with a thick layer of decaying leaves and branches (duff). Sometimes called Pine Vole, which is somewhat of a misnomer since this species doesn't spend much time in coniferous habitats. The Latin species name *pinetorum* is also misleading because it refers to a pine habitat as well. Why these names have been applied is unknown. The genus *Microtus* is Greek and refers to the small ears that are common to this genus.

The small body and ears, tiny eyes and large front claws suit it well for an underground (fossorial) life of digging. Digs out areas to cache food for consumption later.

The chestnut color, small size and unique tail help to identify the Woodland Vole. Its bicolored tail is unlike that of all other vole species, gradually changing from dark above to light below.

Can be semi-colonial, with several families sharing a single nest chamber. Doesn't seem to have the "peak and crash" population cycles common to the other vole species. Owls, hawks, coyotes, foxes, minks and other predators all depend on these critters for a constant source of food.

Meadow Vole
Microtus pennsylvanicus

Family: Rats and Mice (Muridae)

Size: L 4-5" (10-13 cm); T 1½-2½" (4-6 cm)

Weight: 1-2½ oz. (28-71 g)

Description: Overall dark gray with rusty red highlights and peppered with black. Gray chest and belly. Short round snout. Ears small, but visible. Tail is dark above, light below.

Origin/Age: native; 1-2 years

Compare: Prairie Vole (pg. 149) is similar, but has a shorter tail. Southern Red-backed Vole (pg. 137) has a redder coat and shorter tail. Both of these voles have limited ranges in Georgia. Woodland Vole (pg. 141) has a bicolored tail that gradually changes from dark above to light below, not like the sharply demarcated tail of Meadow Vole.

Habitat: wet grassy meadows and fields, moist woodland edges

Home: ball-shaped nest with a hollow center, made of dried grass, usually underneath a log or rock; lives above ground and underground; maintains a system of trails and tunnels

Food: herbivore; green grass, seeds, sedges

Sounds: inconsequential; chatters, grinds teeth and drums hind feet on the ground when threatened

Breeding: Apr-Nov mating, sometimes will mate in winter; 21 days gestation

Young: 3-10 pups (average 7) up to 15 times per year; weaned at about 2 weeks

145

Signs: well-worn runways in the grass; piles of freshly cut grass stacked up along runways

Activity: diurnal, nocturnal; active year-round, often active 24 hours a day with several hours of rest followed by several hours of activity, less active on nights with a full moon

scat

Tracks: hind paw ¾" (2 cm) long with 5 toes, forepaw ½" (1 cm) long with 4 toes; individual tracks are indistinguishable and create a single groove

Stan's Notes: This vole makes its home in the northern half of Georgia. Also called Salt Marsh Vole. At times mistakenly called Meadow Mouse or Field Mouse, but this is not a mouse; does not enter homes like mice. Fares well in abandoned farmlands and most places that are moist and have thick grass, including fields.

While many other small mammals include insects in their diet, this is one of the few small animals that is strictly vegetarian.

Thought to have a social system in which females are territorial, with males moving freely in and around female territories. Tends to be solitary during the breeding season and gathers in non-breeding groups in winter. During periods of activity, it maintains runways, feeds, finds a mate and marks territory with urine and feces.

pups

The most prolific mammal on earth by far, with the female able to reproduce at 3 weeks. Female has a postpartum estrus, which allows her to mate almost immediately after giving birth.

This species is preyed upon by many larger mammals and birds when the population is abundant. Population cycles swing up and down every 2-5 years; unknown why or how this happens.

Prairie Vole
Microtus ochrogaster

Family: Rats and Mice (Muridae)

Size: L 4-5" (10-13 cm); T 1-1½" (2.5-4 cm)

Weight: 1¼-2 oz. (35-57 g)

Description: Gray brown to yellow brown above, lighter gray below. Gray-tipped or black-tipped hair gives it a grizzled appearance. Short round snout. Short bicolored tail, dark above, lighter below. Ears are small and barely visible. Only 5 toe pads on the hind feet.

Origin/Age: native; 1-2 years

Compare: Southern Red-backed Vole (pg. 137) is smaller, has a rusty red back, silvery white belly and slightly longer tail. Prairie Vole has 5 toe pads on its hind feet unlike other voles, which have 6.

Habitat: prairies, dry grassy meadows, dry fields

Home: ball-shaped nest with a hollow center, made from dried grass

Food: herbivore, insectivore; seeds, green grass, roots, tubers, insects

Sounds: inconsequential; rarely, if ever, heard

Breeding: May-Oct mating; 21 days gestation; most breed only a couple times each year

Young: 3-5 pups; born naked with pink skin, brown fur appears at about 2 days, crawls at about 5 days, eats solid food at about 12 days, leaves mother after only 2-3 weeks

runway

Signs: extensive system of aboveground, well-worn runways where grass is cut and removed, runways can be packed bare soil or lined with grass clippings; scat rarely seen

Activity: diurnal, nocturnal; active year-round, spends much of its time underground in dens, active in 4-hour cycles with more daytime activity in winter and less during hot summer months

Tracks: hind paw ¾-1" (2-2.5 cm) long with 5 toes, forepaw ½" (1 cm) long with 4 toes; individual tracks are indistinguishable and create a single groove

Stan's Notes: A vole of dry prairies. Since this is a rare habitat in Georgia, the Prairie Vole is less common than the Woodland Vole (pg. 141) and Meadow Vole (pg. 145). Prairie Vole lives in dryer areas, while Meadow Vole takes the wetter habitats. Well adapted to life on the prairie, it creates burrows and maintains an extensive surface runway system. Rarely a problem to people. Will often cache extra seeds in its burrow system. A good source of food for hawks, owls, foxes and other larger mammals.

Range stretches from Ohio in the East, west across the plains to Montana, south to Oklahoma and back to the northwestern corner of Georgia. Local populations can range from a few dozen to several hundred individuals per acre.

Like the other voles and lemmings, it has a large pouch (cecum) at the beginning of its colon. The cecum contains microscopic bacteria (microflora), which help break down cellulose, the main component in plant material.

Starts to breed at 4 weeks. A monogamous vole, with females producing small litters. Young apparently produce an ultrasonic sound that helps their parents find them in the dark.

During drought, females do not ovulate and reproduction drops. Reproduces throughout the year with peaks occurring from May through August. Specific peaks appear to tie to the availability of moisture and increased production of grass, which shelters and feeds these mammals. Populations peak every 2-4 years. These cycles are not well understood and are still being studied.

151

Round-tailed Muskrat
Neofiber alleni

Family: Rats and Mice (Muridae)

Size: L 6-10" (15-25 cm); T 5-7" (13-18 cm)

Weight: 6-12 oz. (170-340 g)

Description: Glossy dark brown fur, lighter on belly. Round, dark naked tail, covered with scales. Long tail, but not as long as the head and body combined. Small round ears, well hidden in dense fur. Tiny eyes. Large webbed hind feet. Long claws.

Origin/Age: native; 3-10 years

Compare: Muskrat (pg. 157) is much larger and more common and widespread in Georgia. Round-tailed has a longer, thinner tail than American Beaver (pg. 165), which is much larger and has a large flat tail, not a round tail. Much smaller than the Nutria (pg. 161), which has a large rounded head and blunt snout.

Habitat: ponds, lakes, ditches, small rivers, streams

Home: small den, called a lodge, made of long grasses and other soft green (herbaceous) plant material, 1-2 underwater entrances, 1 chamber, not made with mud or woody plants

Food: herbivore; aquatic plants, maidencane grass and cattail shoots, roots and rhizomes

Sounds: inconsequential; squeaking, chewing sounds can be heard when feeding on a feeding platform

Breeding: year-round mating; 25-30 days gestation

Young: 1-4 offspring 3-4 times per year; born naked with eyes closed, swims at about 2 weeks, weaned at about 3 weeks

153

Signs: well-worn trails through vegetation along a shore near a muskrat lodge, feeding platform made of floating plant material, 24" square (154.8 sq. cm), usually strewn with partially eaten plants; lodge made of fine grasses and other cut vegetation

Activity: nocturnal, crepuscular; active all year, doesn't hibernate, can be seen during the day

Tracks: hind paw 1½-2" (4-5 cm) long with 5 toes and a long heel, forepaw 1" (1.5 cm) with 5 toes spread evenly; hind paws fall near or onto fore prints (direct register) when walking, often obliterating the forepaw tracks; prints may show only 4 toes since the fifth toe is not well formed, often has a tail drag mark

Stan's Notes: A member of the Voles and Lemmings (Arvicolinae) subfamily, which is in the Rats and Mice (Muridae) family. Native only to Georgia and Florida. Not very common in Georgia, found in isolated pockets in southeastern and southern parts of the state. Round-tailed is a close relative of the Muskrat (pg. 157), which is a much more widespread species across the United States.

The musky odor (most evident in males during breeding season) emanating from two glands of its rat-like tail is the reason for the "Muskrat" common name. Some people say the common name is a derivation of the Algonquian Indian word *musquash*, which sounds somewhat like "muskrat."

A mostly aquatic mammal, the Round-tailed Muskrat is highly suited to living in water. It has a waterproof coat that protects it from water. Partially webbed hind feet and a fringe of hair along each toe help the muskrat propel itself. The tail, which is round, also helps with forward motion and is used as a rudder. A good swimmer; swims backward and sideways with ease. Able to stay submerged for up to 15 minutes. Its mouth can close behind the front teeth only, allowing the animal to cut vegetation free while it is submerged. Surfaces to eat. May store some roots and tubers in mud below the water to consume during times of drought.

Lives with other muskrats in small groups, but there is no social structure; individuals act mainly on their own. Becomes sexually mature the first spring after its birth.

Lodges are built with aquatic grasses, with a flat platform inside. Two entrance/exit holes lead into the water below. A muskrat lodge is not like a beaver lodge, which is constructed with woody plant material and mud. While there is only one beaver lodge per lake or stream, there are often several muskrat lodges in a body of water. Does not defecate in the lodge, so the interior living space is kept remarkably clean.

Muskrat
Ondatra zibethicus

Family: Rats and Mice (Muridae)

Size: L 8-12" (20-30 cm); T 7-12" (18-30 cm)

Weight: 1-4 lb. (.5-1.8 kg)

Description: Glossy dark brown, lighter on the sides and belly. Long naked tail, covered with scales and slightly vertically flattened (taller than it is wide). Small round ears. Tiny eyes.

Origin/Age: native; 3-10 years

Compare: Round-tailed Muskrat (pg. 153) is much smaller and has a round tail. Nutria (pg. 161) is much larger, with a large head and blunt snout. The American Beaver (pg. 165) has a large flat tail.

Habitat: ponds, lakes, ditches, small rivers, streams

Home: small den, called a lodge, made of cattail leaves and other soft green (herbaceous) plant material, 1-2 underwater entrances, often has 1 chamber, sometimes a burrow in a lakeshore, larger dens may have 2 chambers with separate occupants

Food: herbivore, carnivore to a much lesser extent; aquatic plants, roots, cattail and bulrush shoots, roots and rhizomes; also eats dead fish, crayfish, clams, snails and baby birds

Sounds: inconsequential; chewing sounds can be heard when feeding above water on a feeding platform

Breeding: Apr-Aug mating, year-round in some areas; 25-30 days gestation

Young: 6-7 offspring 2-3 times per year; born naked with eyes closed, swims at about 2 weeks, weaned at about 3 weeks

157

swimming

lodge

Signs: well-worn trails through vegetation along a shore near a muskrat lodge, feeding platform made of floating plant material, 24" square (154.8 sq. cm), usually strewn with partially eaten cattails and other plants; lodge made of mud and cut vegetation, occasionally many lodges will dot the surface of a shallow lake

Activity: nocturnal, crepuscular; active all year, doesn't hibernate

Tracks: hind paw 2½-3½" (6-9 cm) long with 5 toes and a long heel, forepaw about half the size with 5 toes spread evenly; hind paws fall near or onto fore prints (direct register) when walking, often obliterating the forepaw tracks; prints may show only 4 toes since the fifth toe is not well formed, often has a tail drag mark

Stan's Notes: A member of the Voles and Lemmings (Arvicolinae) subfamily, which is in the Rats and Mice (Muridae) family. Native only to North America; introduced all over the world. The musky odor (most evident in males during breeding season) emanating from two glands near the base of its rat-like tail is the reason for the common name. Some say the common name is a derivation of the Algonquian Indian word *musquash*, which sounds somewhat like "muskrat."

Mostly aquatic, the muskrat is highly suited to living in water. It has a waterproof coat that protects it from frigid temperatures. Partially webbed hind feet and a fringe of hair along each toe help propel the animal. The tail, which is slightly flattened vertically, also helps with forward motion and is used as a rudder. Its mouth can close behind the front teeth only, allowing the animal to cut vegetation free while it is submerged.

A good swimmer that swims backward and sideways with ease. Able to stay submerged for up to 15 minutes. Surfaces to eat. May store some roots and tubers in mud below the water to consume during times of drought.

It lives with other muskrats in small groups, but there is no social structure and individuals act mainly on their own. Becomes sexually mature the first spring after its birth.

Lodge building seems to concentrate in the fall. Not all muskrats construct a mound-type lodge. Many dig a burrow in a shore. A muskrat lodge is not like a beaver lodge, which is made with woody plant material. There is only one beaver lodge per lake or stream, while there are often several muskrat lodges in a body of water. Does not defecate in the lodge, so the interior living space of the lodge is kept remarkably clean.

Overcrowding can occur in fall and winter, causing individuals to travel great distances in spring to establish new homes. Many muskrats are killed when crossing roads during this season.

Nutria
Myocaster coypus

Family: Myocastorids (Myocastoridae)

Size: L 15-37" (38-94 cm); T 11-18" (28-45 cm)

Weight: 14-18 lb. (6.3-8.1 kg)

Description: Light to dark brown with gold highlights. Slightly lighter belly. Long, round scaly tail. Round dark ears, long stout snout, small eyes and white chin Large yellow incisors. Short legs. Female has a row of mammae on each side of the back.

Origin/Age: non-native; 3-10 years

Compare: Round-tailed Muskrat (pg. 153) and Muskrat (pg. 157) are smaller, with smaller snouts. The American Beaver (pg. 165) has a large flat tail.

Habitat: ponds, wetlands, ditches, small rivers

Home: shallow burrow, single chamber, often in a wetland bank, sometimes in a tangle of tree roots, entrance above water line; nest of cattail leaves and other soft green plant (herbaceous) materials on land or in thick vegetation near the water; sometimes takes over an old beaver or muskrat lodge

Food: herbivore; aquatic plants, roots, cattail and bulrush shoots, sedges, roots, rhizomes; along the coast it feeds on shellfish

Sounds: chorus of pig-like grunts heard along wetlands at dusk; makes chewing sounds when eating on a feeding platform

Breeding: year-round mating; 125-135 days gestation

Young: 2-11 (usually 5) offspring 2-3 times per year; born fully furred with eyes open, able to move around and feed within hours

161

Signs: well-worn trails through vegetation along wetlands, feeding platform constructed of floating plant material, 24" square (154.8 sq. cm), usually strewn with partially eaten cattails and other plants; nests made of cut vegetation; elongated scat found on feeding platforms or in shallow water

Activity: nocturnal; active year-round, does not hibernate

Tracks: hind paw 4½-5½" (10.5-14 cm) long with 5 toes (webbed) and a long heel, forepaw about half the size with 5 toes spread evenly; hind paws fall near fore prints when walking; hind prints may show only 4 toes since the fifth toe is not well formed and off to the side; may have a tail drag mark

Stan's Notes: A large aquatic rodent, nearly the size of a beaver. Introduced from South America in 1889 for its high-quality fur. Raised on ranches for its fur, it eventually escaped into the wild due to a variety of reasons. During the 1940s, the fur industry collapsed and many others were released into the wild.

Originally from semiaquatic habitats in southern Chile and farther south in Tierra del Fuego. One of the few mammals that can thrive in fresh water and saltwater. Today in Georgia it has spread north from Florida. Reported in 22 states total, but occurs mainly in Gulf coast states.

An excellent swimmer, with only its ears, eyes and nostrils visible above the surface. Can dive and remained submerged for long periods of time to evade predators.

Competes with the smaller, local native muskrat species for the limited suitable habitats such as wetlands. Lives in a variety of homes, including burrows that it excavates itself or takes from others. Feeds, loafs, gives birth and escapes from predators on circular platforms built from vegetation, which are often mistaken for muskrat houses.

Breeds year-round and quickly overpopulates. Once established, it often eats most of the aquatic vegetation, causing extensive damage to wetlands. Eats all of the native vegetation that holds wetland soils together. A nocturnal animal, so usually only the damage is seen, not the culprit.

Considered an invasive species in the United States. Previously sold as a "natural" control for noxious weeds, this unfortunately also helped extend its range in nearly all states where it occurs. Efforts to control the population include government-sponsored programs to hunt and trap the animal. While South Americans enjoy its meat, efforts here to market it for consumption did not catch on with the public.

American Beaver
Castor canadensis

Family: Beavers (Castoridae)

Size: L 3-4' (.9-1.2 m); T 7-14" (18-36 cm)

Weight: 20-60 lb. (9-27 kg)

Description: Reddish brown fur. Body often darker than head. Large, flat, naked black tail, covered with scales. Small round ears. Large, exposed orange incisors. Tiny eyes.

Origin/Age: native; 10-15 years

Compare: Round-tailed Muskrat (pg. 153) and Muskrat (pg. 157) are much smaller, with long thin tails. Nutria (pg. 161) is smaller and has a long snout and long scaly tail. Look for a large flat tail to help identify the American Beaver.

Habitat: rivers, streams, ponds, lakes, ditches, wherever trees and water are present

Home: den, called a lodge, hollow inside with holes on top for ventilation, 1-2 underwater entrances; beavers that live on rivers often dig burrows in riverbanks rather than constructing dens

Food: herbivore; soft bark, inner bark, aquatic plants, green leaves

Sounds: loud slap created by hitting the surface of water with the tail before diving when alarmed, chewing or gnawing sounds when feeding or felling trees

Breeding: Jan-Mar mating; 120 days gestation

Young: 1-8 kits once per year; about 1 lb. (.5 kg); born well furred with eyes open, able to swim within 1 week

tail slap

lodge

scat

Signs: dam and lodge made from large woody branches can indicate current or former activity since structures remain well after the beaver has moved on or been killed, chewed tree trunks with large amounts of wood chips at the base of trees, flattened paths through vegetation leading to and from a lake; oval pellets, 1" (2.5 cm) long, containing sawdust-like material and bark, scat seldom on land

Activity: nocturnal, crepuscular; active year-round

Tracks: hind paw 5" (13 cm) long with 5 toes pointing forward and a long narrow heel, forepaw 3" (7.5 cm) with 5 splayed toes; wide tail drag mark often wipes out paw prints

Stan's Notes: This is the largest native rodent in Georgia. Body is well suited for swimming. Valves close off the ears and nostrils when underwater, and a clear membrane covers the eyes. Can remain submerged up to 15 minutes. Webbed toes on hind feet help it swim as fast as 6 mph (10 km/h). Special lips seal the mouth yet leave the front incisors exposed, allowing it to carry branches in its mouth without water getting inside. At the lodge, it eats the soft bark of smaller branches the same way we eat corn on the cob. Doesn't eat the interior wood. Stores branches for later use by sticking them in mud on a lake or river bottom. A specialized claw on each hind foot is split like a comb and used for grooming.

Builds a dam to back up a large volume of water, creating a pond. Cuts trees at night by gnawing trunks. Uses larger branches to construct the dam and lodge. Cuts smaller branches and twigs of felled trees into 6-foot (1.8 m) sections. Dam repair is triggered by the sound of moving water, not by sight. Most repair activity takes place at night.

Given its genus name *Castor* for the pungent castor oil that it secretes from glands near the base of its tail. Uses castor to mark territories or boundaries called castor mounds. Castor oil from this gland is not the same castor oil from plants used in medicines.

Monogamous and mates for life. However, will take a new mate if partner is lost. Can live up to 20 years in captivity. Young remain with parents through their first winter. They help cut and store a winter food source and maintain the dam while parents raise another set of young. Young disperse at 2 years.

No other mammal except people changes the environment as much as beavers. Frogs, turtles and many bird species, including ducks, herons and egrets, benefit from the newly created habitat. Beavers have made a comeback in Georgia after being killed off by excessive trapping and hunting. Their return has been on their own; no program was established for their reintroduction.

Big Brown Bat
Eptesicus fuscus

Family: Bats (Vespertilionidae)

Size: L 2-3" (5-7.5 cm); T 1½-2" (4-5 cm)

Weight: ½-⁹⁄₁₀ oz. (14-26 g)

Description: Brown to yellow brown fur. Dark, membranous naked wings and tail. Lighter brown belly. Dark, oval naked ears with a short, fleshy, curved projection (tragus). Bright black eyes. Pointed snout.

Origin/Age: native; 15-20 years

Compare: Nearly identical to Little Brown Bat (pg. 172), which winter roosts in caves; Big Brown tends to winter roost in buildings. Look for a plain brown back with black ears and face to help identify.

Habitat: wide variety such as deciduous forests, suburban and urban areas, farmlands

Home: walls and attics of homes, churches, barns and other buildings year-round, maternity colonies also in hollow trees, will winter in mines, tunnels and caves, but little is known about these sites

Food: insectivore; small to large flying insects

Sounds: fast series of high-pitched clicking noises, high-pitched squeaks of pups calling persistently for their mother can be heard up to 30' (9.1 m) away

Breeding: Aug-Sep mating before hibernation; 60-62 days gestation; sperm stored in the reproductive tract until the spring following mating

Young: 1-2 (usually 2) pups once per year, May to July; born breach, naked with eyes closed, weighs one-third the weight of the mother, flies at 28-35 days

169

Signs: piles of dark brown-to-black scat under roosting sites

Activity: nocturnal; active only on warm dry nights, comes out approximately 30 minutes after sunset, feeds until full, roosts the rest of night, returns to daytime roost before sunrise

scat

Tracks: none

Stan's Notes: One of 16 bat species in Georgia. A common bat in many habitats from forests to cities and the country. Seen across North America from Maine to Washington and southward as far as Central America.

Studies show that this species feeds on many crop and forest pests and insects, making it one of America's most beneficial animals and very desirable to have around. It is a fast-flying bat, reaching speeds of up to 25 mph (40 km/h), with an erratic flight pattern, evident as it swoops and dives for mosquitoes, beetles and other flying insects. Often forages over rivers and lakes, beneath street-lights or wherever large groups of flying insects congregate. Emits a high-frequency (27-48 kHz) sound (inaudible to people) to locate prey and listens for returning echoes (echolocation). Most of these bats catch and eat one insect every three seconds, consuming $\frac{1}{10}$ ounce (3 g) per hour. During summer, when rapidly growing pups demand increasing amounts of milk, a lactating female can consume up to $\frac{7}{10}$ ounce (20 g) of insects every night, which is nearly equal to her own body weight.

Rarely winters in caves, preferring to hibernate alone or in small groups. Males are generally solitary during spring and summer.

Females will gather in maternity colonies of up to 75 individuals. Loyal to these maternal roosts, females return to them year after year. Approximately 80 percent of females give birth to two pups at the maternal roosts in spring and early summer.

A mother does not carry her pups during flight, but leaves them clinging to the roost until she returns. Holds pups to her chest under a wing to nurse. Recognizes young by their vocalizations.

Homeowners frequently discover these bats when remodeling or adding onto their homes during winter months. Any unwanted bat found in homes should be professionally moved or removed to avoid hurting the animal.

Similar species on next page 171

There are 43 bat species in the United States, with 16 species in Georgia. The order of bats, called Chiroptera, means "hand wing" and refers to the elongated fingers that all bats have with thin membranous skin stretched between. No other mammal besides the bat has the ability to fly.

All bats are nocturnal, with small eyes and large ears. They use high-frequency ultrasonic sounds (outside the hearing range of people) to avoid obstacles and find insect prey while in flight.

Bats live in all regions around the world except for polar regions. Several bat species roost in caves in Georgia. These are usually females giving birth to pups.

Little Brown Bat
1½-2"

Eastern Pipistrelle
2-2¼"

Evening Bat
1¾-2¼"

Eastern Small-footed Myotis 2-2½"

Northern Myotis
2-2½"

Brazilian Free-tailed Bat 2¼-2½"

Silver-haired Bat
2-3"

Eastern Red Bat
2-3"

Indiana Bat
1¾-3½"

Hoary Bat
2-4"

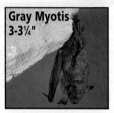
Gray Myotis
3-3¼"

Southeastern Bat 3¼-3⅞"

Rafinesque's Big-eared Bat 3⅞-4¼"

Northern Yellow Bat 4-4½"

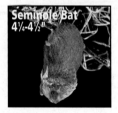
Seminole Bat 4¼-4½"

Eastern Chipmunk
Tamias striatus

Family: Squirrels (Sciuridae)

Size: L 6-8" (15-20 cm); T 3-4" (7.5-10 cm)

Weight: 3-5 oz. (85-142 g)

Description: Overall reddish brown with a single white stripe bordered by 2 dark stripes on each side running from nose to rump. Stripes are less prominent on face. Chin, chest and belly are pale white to gray. Reddish brown rump. Reddish brown tail, half the length of body.

Origin/Age: native; 2-4 years

Compare: Eastern Gray Squirrel (pg. 187) is gray and lacks stripes. Southeastern Pocket Gopher (pg. 199) is larger, lacks stripes and is mainly underground.

Habitat: deciduous and coniferous forests, forest edges, near stone walls, rock piles or human dwellings

Home: burrow with several round entrance holes, each 2" (5 cm) wide with no excavated dirt, can be as long as 10' (3 m) and as deep as 4-5' (1.2-1.5 m) with several chambers for sleeping, storing food and waste, may nest in tree cavity; male and female construct and maintain separate burrows

Food: omnivore; seeds, fruit, nuts, insects, buds, fungi, flowers, frogs, baby birds, bird eggs, small snakes

Sounds: very trilling "chip" note repeated over and over, lower pitched "chuck-chuck-chuck" sound may last several minutes and echo through the woods

Breeding: Mar-Apr mating; 28-30 days gestation

Young: up to 7 offspring 1-2 times a year in May or June

cheek pouch

burrow entrance

Signs: piles of cracked seeds and acorns and other food on a log or large rock; oblong dark brown pellets, ⅛" (.3 cm) long, often not seen and not key in identifying this species

Activity: diurnal; peak activity in the morning and evening, no activity on cold, windy or rainy days

Tracks: hind paw 1¼-1½" (3-4 cm) long with 5 toes, forepaw with 4 toes is about half the size of hind paw; 1 set of 4 tracks; hind paws fall in front of fore prints; tracks rarely seen since it lives in a dry rocky habitat

Stan's Notes: Seen mostly in the northern half of Georgia. Range extends from Minnesota to New England and south to the Gulf coast. The Latin genus *Tamias* means "storer" and refers to its habit of storing large amounts of food in preparation for winter.

Known for loud vocalizations, which almost always are accompanied by a dramatic flick of the tail. Both the male and female vocalize. Usually sounds off while on a favorite perch, where it can survey its territory.

Does not cause damage to gardens, as some think. Burrows help to aerate the ground, and burrow entrances lack dirt mounds. Eats great quantities of seeds that would otherwise germinate in lawns and gardens.

Chipmunks are delightful to watch and many people like to feed them. Can be very tame and tolerant of people. Usually solitary and very commonly seen around human dwellings. Maintains a small territory around the main burrow and will defend it from other "chippies." Has short, dead-end burrows for quick escapes.

Will eat just about anything from plants to animals. Comfortable climbing trees to gather seeds, buds and flowers for food. Can transport large amounts of food, usually seeds, in cheek pouches. Stores large quantities of seeds, nuts and dried berries in an underground cavity connected to its living chambers. Will eat from its cache when it cannot get outside to due weather and in winter.

A light hibernator, waking every 2-3 weeks to eat its stored food. Can occasionally be seen aboveground during warm spells in winter. Common to see it in February, although it usually goes back to sleep until March, when mating season begins.

Breeding season begins a few weeks after it emerges from hibernation, and lasts only a few weeks. Male emerges before female. Female can have two litters per season, but this is not common. Male takes no part in raising young.

Southern Flying Squirrel
Glaucomys volans

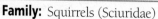

Family: Squirrels (Sciuridae)

Size: L 5-7" (13-18 cm); T 3-5" (7.5-13 cm)

Weight: 1½-2½ oz. (43-71 g)

Description: Light brown-to-gray fur above. White underside. Wide flat tail, gray above and white below. Large, bulging dark eyes. Loose fold of skin between the front and hind legs.

Origin/Age: native; 2-5 years

Compare: The flying squirrel is the only nocturnal squirrel. Can be identified by the wide flat tail and large bulging eyes.

Habitat: large trees, along rivers and streams, woodlands, urban and suburban yards and parks, prefers hummocks where Spanish moss is abundant

Home: nest lined with soft plant material, usually in an old woodpecker hole, sometimes in a nest box or an attic in homes and outbuildings, may build a small round nest of leaves on a tree branch; nest is similar to that of the Eastern Gray Squirrel (pg. 187), only smaller

Food: omnivore; seeds, nuts, carrion, baby mice, baby birds, bird eggs, lichens, mushrooms, fungi

Sounds: faint bird-like calls during the night, young give high-pitched squeaks

Breeding: spring mating; 40 days gestation

Young: 2-6 (average 3) offspring, 2 litters per year

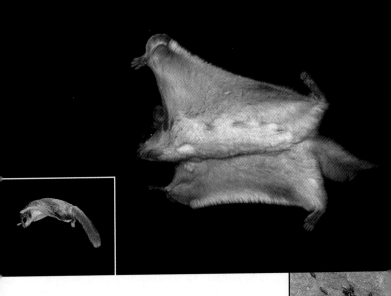

Signs: food has mysteriously disappeared from bird feeders overnight

Activity: nocturnal; active year-round, some-times enters torpor during the very coldest parts of winter

scat

Tracks: hind paw 1" (2.5 cm) long with 5 toes, forepaw ½" (1 cm) long with 4 toes; 1 set of 4 tracks; large landing mark (sitzmark) followed by bounding tracks, with hind paws falling in front of front prints; tracks lead to the base of a tree

Stan's Notes: The flying squirrel is the only nocturnal member of the Squirrels family in Georgia. Its large bulging eyes enable it to see well at night. Common name "Flying" is a misnomer because this animal does not have the capability to fly, only the ability to glide. In part, this is due to a large flap of skin (patagium) that is attached to its front and hind legs and to the sides of its body.

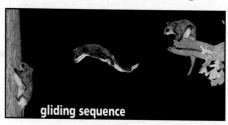

gliding sequence

To glide, the flying squirrel will climb high up in a tree and launch itself forward, extending all four legs out and stretching the skin between its legs (patagium) to make a flat, wing-like airfoil. The flat tail adds some additional lift and acts like a rudder to help maneuver objects while gliding. Most glides are as long as 20-50 feet (6.1-15 m) and terminate at the trunk of another tree. To create an air brake for a soft landing, the squirrel will quickly lift its head and tuck its tail between its hind legs. After landing, it will scamper to the opposite side of the tree trunk, presumably to avoid any flying predators that may be following.

The flying squirrel is the most carnivorous of the tree squirrels, finding, killing and eating small mice, dead flesh (carrion) and even baby birds and bird eggs. It is a gregarious animal, with many individuals living together in a nest.

Young are born helpless with eyes closed. Weaned at 5-7 weeks, they may stay with their mother through their first winter. Most flying squirrels live only 2-5 years, but some have lived as long as 10 years in captivity.

Red Squirrel
Tamiasciurus hudsonicus

Family: Squirrels (Sciuridae)

Size: L 7-9" (18-23 cm); T 4-7" (10-18 cm)

Weight: 5-9 oz. (142-255 g)

Description: Overall rusty red, with brighter red fur on sides. Bright white belly. Distinctive white ring around eyes. Large, fluffy red tail with a black tip. Black line separating the red back from the white belly in summer. Tufted ears in winter.

Origin/Age: native; 2-5 years

Compare: The smallest and the only red tree squirrel.

Habitat: forests, suburban and urban yards, parks

Home: nest (drey) made mainly with grapevine bark and dried leaves, in a tree cavity or burrow, may build a ball-shaped nest or take an Eastern Gray Squirrel (pg. 187) nest

Food: omnivore; pine cone seeds and other seeds, nuts, fruit, acorns, corn, mushrooms; also eats baby birds, bird eggs and carrion

Sounds: loud raspy chatters or wheezy barks when upset or threatened, may bark nonstop for up to an hour, distinctive buzz-like calls given by the male when chasing a female to mate

Breeding: Mar-Apr mating; 33-35 days gestation

Young: 2-5 offspring once per year from April to May; born naked with eyes closed, weaned and on its own after 7-8 weeks

drying mushrooms

scat

Signs: discarded pine cone parts (midden) in a pile on the ground under a tree branch, acorns and other large nuts with a single ragged hole at one end and nutmeat missing

Activity: diurnal; active year-round, but may hole up for a couple days in the nest during very cold, hot or rainy weather

Tracks: hind paw 1½" (4 cm) long with 5 toes, forepaw ¾" (2 cm) long with 4 toes; 1 set of 4 tracks; forepaws fall side by side and behind hind prints

Stan's Notes: Also called Chickaree or Pine Squirrel. Although small in size, Red Squirrel has a big attitude and is well known for chasing away larger Eastern Gray Squirrels (pg. 187) and other small mammals. However, the success of the Red Squirrel is a function of food resources, not feistiness.

Usually associated with pine trees, but can be in non-coniferous habitats. Feeds heavily on pine cone seeds. Cuts the cones from trees and carries them to a specific spot to eat. A large pile of discarded cone parts, known as a midden, accumulates under the perch. Caches up to a bushel of fresh cones in the midden to eat later. Large middens are usually the result of several squirrels using the same favorite perch over time, with one taking over the spot when another dies. Consumes Amanita mushrooms, which are poisonous to people, without ill effects. Hangs mushrooms to dry on tree branches for future consumption.

Like the Eastern Gray Squirrel, it builds leaf nests (dreys), but does not build as many. Sometimes will build its nest in a burrow. May construct a small ball-shaped nest from lichen and grass.

Several males will chase a female on tree branches prior to mating. A male may mate with more than one female, but the female is receptive to mating only once on one day in late winter or spring.

The most seasonally dimorphic of squirrels, molting in late spring and again in early autumn. Black morph and white albinos occur but are quite uncommon, unlike other squirrel species.

The genus *Tamiasciurus* is only in North America and includes one other species, Douglas Squirrel (not shown), which occurs in the Pacific Northwest. The species name *hudsonicus* was given because the Red Squirrel ranges as far north in Canada to Hudson Bay and west across Canada and most of Alaska. In fact, it has one of the widest distributions of any squirrel in North America.

Eastern Gray Squirrel
Sciurus carolinensis

Family: Squirrels (Sciuridae)

Size: L 9-10" (23-25 cm); T 8-9" (20-23 cm)

Weight: 12-24 oz. (340-680 g)

Description: Overall gray or light brown fur with a white chest and belly. Large, bushy gray tail with silver-tipped hairs. Black morph is overall black with a reddish brown shine. Tail may also be reddish brown.

Origin/Age: native; 2-5 years

Compare: Smaller than the Fox Squirrel (pg. 191), which has a rusty tail and black head. Larger than Red Squirrel (pg. 183) and is overall gray.

Habitat: woodlands, suburban and urban yards, parks, mangrove forests, tropical hummocks

Home: leaf nest (drey) in summer, hollow with a single entrance hole and lined with soft plant material, nest is in a tree cavity or old woodpecker hole in winter; male and female live in separate nests in summer, but together in winter

Food: omnivore; nuts, seeds, birdseed, fruit, corn, leaf buds, flowers, mushrooms, inner tree bark, baby birds, bird eggs, small mammals, insects, carrion

Sounds: repeats hoarse, wheezy calls when upset, chatters an alarm call to warn of predators such as cats

Breeding: Jan-Feb mating; 40-45 days gestation

Young: 2-6 offspring once (sometimes twice) per year; born naked with eyes closed, eyes open at about 5 weeks, weaned at about 8-9 weeks, mother pushes young away shortly after weaning

albino

black morph

Signs: acorns and other large nuts split in half with the nutmeat missing, gnaw marks on tree branches stripped of bark, trees that lack new branches with green leaves in early summer

scat

Activity: diurnal; active year-round, feeds late in morning and throughout the day, often rests a couple hours in the afternoon, may stay in nest for several days during very cold or hot periods

Tracks: hind paw 2¼" (5.5 cm) long with 5 toes, forepaw 1" (2.5 cm) long with 4 toes; 1 set of 4 tracks; forepaws fall side by side and behind hind prints

Stan's Notes: Common across Georgia in nearly any place that has trees, especially oaks, which provide acorns. Pockets of black morph squirrels occur throughout the state. The black morph is born black and remains black. The albino morph, an entirely white squirrel with pink eyes, is more rare and does not live as long as the black morph.

Spends most of its life in trees, going to the ground only to feed on fallen nuts and seeds. Buries large amounts of nuts, most only ¼ inch (.6 cm) underground. Studies show about 85 percent of these nuts are recovered. Nuts buried by scientists were recovered at a similar rate, indicating that squirrels find buried food by smell, not memory. Many squirrels "migrate" in years with poor nut crops, moving to find a new home range with adequate food.

During the mating season, males will chase the females. Mating chases are long, with much jumping, bounding and biting.

Leaf nests (dreys) are located away from the main trunk of a tree and are constructed to shed water. A squirrel can have up to seven dreys, which are sometimes used as emergency nests. Usually born in a cavity nest, babies may be moved to a drey when the mother feels threatened. Mothers raise their young alone and move them from nest to nest, perhaps to avoid flea infestations. Studies show that 80 percent die in their first year due to predation by animals that eat squirrels such as coyotes, foxes and hawks.

leaf nest

Considered a nuisance by many because it eats birdseed. Eats a variety of foods, however, including some mushrooms that are poisonous to people. Famous for its ability to access nearly any bird feeder, spending hours, days or weeks devising a way to get the food. An industry has flourished around squirrel-proof feeders.

Sherman's

Fox Squirrel
Sciurus niger

Family: Squirrels (Sciuridae)

Size: L 10-15" (25-38 cm); T 8-13" (20-33 cm)

Weight: 1-2¼ lb. (.5-1 kg)

Description: Highly variable in color. Dark gray to black with orange or white highlights. White ears and nose and occasionally white feet. Large fluffy tail. Can be light gray to orange with a black head and front legs. Other individuals can be all black.

Origin/Age: native; 2-5 years

Compare: Eastern Gray Squirrel (pg. 187) is smaller and lacks a white nose and ears and black face.

Habitat: open woodlands, along rivers and streams, river valleys, yards, parks, golf courses

Home: leaf nest (drey) in summer, up to 24" (61 cm) wide, lined with soft plant material, usually with a side entrance, in a major fork near the main trunk of a tree, nest is in a tree cavity in winter and occupied by several individuals if enough food is available, also used for birthing; may build and use up to 6 nests

Food: omnivore; nuts, corn, pine cone seeds and other seeds, fruit, mushrooms, bird eggs, baby birds, mice, insects, carrion

Sounds: scolding calls similar to those of the Eastern Gray Squirrel, only more hoarse

Breeding: Jan-Feb and Jun-Jul mating; 40-45 days gestation

Young: 2-4 offspring once per year; born with eyes closed, eyes open at about 30 days, leaves mother and on its own at about 3 months

191

Eastern Sherman's

black morph white morph

Signs: large debris pile of split nutshells, whole corncobs and husks strewn about underneath the feeding perch

Activity: diurnal; active year-round, usually begins feeding late in the morning, several hours after sunrise, often active during the middle of the day

Tracks: hind paw 2¾-3" (7-7.5 cm) long with 5 toes, forepaw 1½" (4 cm) long with 4 toes; 1 set of 4 tracks; forepaws fall side by side and behind hind prints

Stan's Notes: Fox Squirrels in Georgia have at least some black, hence the species name *niger*. "Fox" refers to the fox-like fluffy tail.

The Fox Squirrel is the largest tree squirrel, with 10 subspecies in the United States. The dark variety, known as Sherman's, and the rusty Eastern (*S. niger*) are found throughout Georgia. Black morphs are uncommon throughout the state, and white morphs are rare. Both are protected and may not be hunted in Georgia.

Sometimes takes food to its favorite spot to eat. The home range is 10 times larger than that of Eastern Gray Squirrels (pg. 187)–up to 50 acres (20 ha)–so only several Fox Squirrels are found in any given area. Found in a variety of forested habitats, mainly in open pine woodlands, with oak and cypress trees along rivers and streams. In parks and golf courses it is sometimes fed by people. Seen in dry pine-oak woods throughout Georgia.

The tannin in the acorns it eats is highly toxic to tapeworms and roundworms; thus, Fox Squirrels rarely host these parasites. Other than acorns, pine seeds are the favorite food.

leaf nest

Several males "chase" one female prior to mating, following her throughout the day. Females will mate with more than one male. Mating occurs in late winter and again in midsummer. Females begin to breed at 1 year and produce only a single litter per year.

Woodchuck
Marmota monax

Family: Squirrels (Sciuridae)

Size: L 18-28" (45-71 cm); T 3-6" (7.5-15 cm)

Weight: 4-14 lb. (1.8-6.3 kg)

Description: Various shades of red to brown or gray to black. Hair is tipped with gray, yellow or black, giving it a salt-and-pepper appearance. Wide body with very short legs. Small round ears and dark eyes. Dark brown or black feet. Large, bushy dark tail. Male slightly larger than female.

Origin/Age: native; 2-4 years

Compare: The Woodchuck's wide body and very short legs make it easy to identify.

Habitat: fields, pastures, meadows, around homes and other buildings, woodland edges, woodlands

Home: den, often underneath a building or steps, up to 30' (9.1 m) long and down to 5' (1.5 m) deep; entrance is 8-12" (20-30 cm) wide, often with large dirt piles outside, almost always has 1-2 additional escape entrances, which lack dirt piles

Food: herbivore; green vegetation, leaf buds, grasses; especially likes dandelions

Sounds: sharp, whistle-like alarm call

Breeding: Mar-Apr mating; 30 days gestation

Young: 3-7 offspring once per year in May or June; born naked with eyes closed, opens eyes and crawls at about 4 weeks, weaned at about 6 weeks, will disperse to own area at 8-10 weeks

hibernating

scat

Signs: wide holes underneath buildings and in hillsides, leaves and flowers that have been chewed off neatly; small, round brown pellets, ¼-½" (.6-1 cm) wide, deposited into special underground chambers

Activity: diurnal; most active in the morning and evening, especially during the hot summer months, spends many hours feeding on grass

Tracks: hind paw 3-3¾" (7.5-9.5 cm) long with 5 toes, forepaw with 4 toes is slightly smaller than hind paw; tracks are not very common since the animal does not come out when there is snow on the ground, when conditions are muddy or in wet weather

Stan's Notes: The Woodchuck is a type of marmot and is the largest member of the Squirrel family in Georgia. The common name "Woodchuck" is said to come from the Cree Indian word *wuchak*, which was used to describe several small brown animals. The animal for which Groundhog Day is named, it is also known as Groundhog or Whistle Pig. These common names come from its stout stature and sharp whistle-like call it gives when alarmed.

Solitary except for mating and when a mother raises her young. All other marmots, most of which occur in western states, are colonial. It is rarely seen feeding far from the den entrance, since retreating into the den is its major line of defense. Will wait at the entrance until danger has

juvenile

passed, then slowly returns to feeding. Unlike the common name suggests, the Woodchuck does not eat wood, but feeds instead on green vegetation such as grass and especially likes dandelions. Will climb small trees in spring to eat the green buds.

Feeds during the summer, adding body fat to sustain itself throughout hibernation. Will lay curled up in a ball with its head between its front legs. A true hibernator, its body temperature drops from 90 °F (32 °C) to 40 °F (4 °C), breathing slows to once every 6 minutes and heart rate decreases from 75 to 4 beats per minute.

Has a large tunnel system, which is often used by other mammals such as cottontails, raccoons and opossums. Usually will have separate summer and winter dens. The winter den is often in a woodland. It has a single entrance, and the hibernation chamber is lined with dried grass and leaves.

The female Woodchuck breeds at 1 year of age. She may use a separate chamber in the den to give birth.

Southeastern Pocket Gopher
Geomys pinetis

Family: Pocket Gophers (Geomyidae)

Size: L 9-13" (23-33 cm); T 2-4" (5-10 cm)

Weight: 4½-7 oz. (128-198 g)

Description: Dark brown to reddish brown upper body. Belly gray to off-white. Body widest at the shoulders. Short dense fur. Short powerful legs. Pink feet. Extremely large front feet with very long claws. Small round ears. Tiny eyes. Naked tail.

Origin/Age: native; 2-5 years

Compare: The only gopher species found in Georgia. Look for the large front claws and short legs to help differentiate it from tree squirrels (pp. 183-191). The Eastern Chipmunk (pg. 175) is seen mostly in the northern half of Georgia and has stripes. Larger than any of the voles (pp. 137-149) and has a longer tail. The Norway Rat (pg. 129) has a narrow pointed head and very long tail.

Habitat: loose sandy soils, fields, prairies, meadows, roadside ditches, golf courses, cemeteries, pastures

Home: network of tunnels, usually with 2 levels, some about 6" (15 cm) deep, used for gathering food, deeper tunnels down to 6' (1.8 m) are used for nesting and raising young

Food: herbivore; roots, bulbs, rhizomes

Sounds: inconsequential; rarely, if ever, heard

Breeding: Feb-Mar and Jul-Aug mating; 50-55 days gestation

Young: 1-3 offspring 1-2 times per year; born naked and helpless with eyes closed

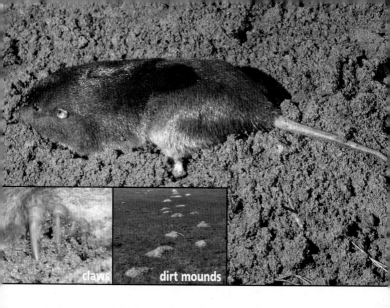

claws

dirt mounds

Signs: mounds of excess dirt as wide as 24" (61 cm) resulting from tunneling, ridges of dirt pushed up from tunneling; opening to tunnel system only rarely seen (would require digging into a dirt mound)

Activity: diurnal, nocturnal; active year-round, alternates several hours of activity with several hours of sleep

Tracks: forepaw 1-1½" (2.5-4 cm) long, hind paw ¾" (2 cm), both with well-defined claw marks; spends almost all of its time in its underground tunnel system, so tracks are rarely seen

Stan's Notes: There are 35 gopher species, all unique to North America. Southeastern Pocket Gopher is the only one that occurs in Georgia.

Specialized fur-lined cheek pouches or "pockets" give the pocket gopher its common name. Able to stuff large amounts of food or nesting material in its pouches, which extend from its cheeks to front shoulders. Cleans the pouches by turning them inside out.

Digs with its powerful front legs and long sharp claws, preferring loose sandy soils. Specialized lips close behind its large incisor teeth, keeping dirt out of the mouth while it digs. Incisor teeth are coated with enamel and grow throughout its life. Must gnaw on hard objects to keep its teeth sharp and prevent them from growing too large and rendering them useless. Sensitive hair/bristles (vibrissae) on the wrists and various parts of the body help it feel its way through tunnels. A narrow pelvis enables it to turn around while in tunnels. Its fur can lay forward or backward and allows the animal to back up without slowing down. Has a good sense of smell, but poor hearing and eyesight. Holds its eyes tightly closed when tunneling to keep out sand. Able to tolerate low levels of oxygen and high levels of carbon dioxide which are a result of living in tunnels that are sealed off from the outside air.

Lives entirely underground. Feeds on roots and bulbs of different plant species, depending upon the season and availability, and stores some food in underground chambers. Has been known to pull entire plants underground by the roots. Solitary except to mate, with only one animal living in a set of tunnels and mounds.

Has adapted well to human activity, often taking up residence in open grassy yards. This animal is very beneficial to the land since its digging aerates the soil, which allows for better drainage and nutrient mixing. However, it can be destructive to gardens and fields because it eats many of the plants.

Marsh Rabbit
Sylvilagus palustris

Family: Rabbits and Hares (Leporidae)

Size: L 13-17" (33-43 cm); T 1-1½" (2.5-4 cm)

Weight: 2-3½ lb. (.9-1.6 kg)

Description: Overall rusty brown or reddish brown short hair (pelage), grizzled with black. Paler on the sides to gray or white on belly. Small head compared with the body. Short, broad rounded ears, sparsely haired. Pale eye-ring. Short legs and small feet, all rusty red. Short puffy tail. Some individuals have a tiny amount of gray beneath. Large dark eyes.

Origin/Age: native; 1-3 years

Compare: Smaller than Swamp Rabbit (pg. 215), which is darker and occurs in the western half of Georgia. Eastern Cottontail (pg. 211) has larger, narrower ears and is overall gray with a rusty red nape.

Habitat: river bottoms, coastal marshes, mangroves, lowlands, wetlands, along streams, just about any other place with shallow standing water

Home: shallow nest, lined with soft plant material and fur, covered with dry grasses and leaves under a fallen log at the base of a tree

Food: herbivore; grass, other green plants, woody plants

Sounds: loud high-pitched scream or squeal when caught by a fox, coyote or raptor, thumps its feet

Breeding: Feb-Sep mating; 28-37 days gestation; starts to breed during the first year

Young: 2-4 offspring 3-5 times per year; born furred, with eyes and ears closed, opening within 4-5 days

Signs: runways in tall grass leading to and from wetlands, small woody twigs and branches near the ground are cleanly cut off and at an angle; pea-sized, round, dry, woody, light brown pellets

Activity: nocturnal, crepuscular; can also be seen during the day, often very active during February and March when males fight to breed with females

Tracks: hind paw 3½-4" (9-10 cm) long, forepaw ½" (1 cm) long, small and round, long nails; 1 set of 4 tracks; forepaws fall one in front of the other behind hind prints, front nails are often seen in tracks

Stan's Notes: Very similar to Eastern Cottontail (pg. 211), which is widespread and very common. Nowhere is the Appalachian Cottontail common. Considered uncommon or rare everywhere in its range.

A secretive forest-dwelling rabbit species. Tends to run in a zig-zag pattern when running from predators. Females are slightly larger than the males. Usually solitary, but may get together for some social behaviors, such as grouping into hierarchies, with dominant individuals cajoling the submissive rabbits.

Possibly the only cottontail rabbit to feed on coniferous needles regularly. Expels two types of fecal pellets: hard round brown and soft green. The greenish pellets contain leftover digestible vegetation, and high amounts of protein and vitamin B produced by intestinal bacteria. These soft pellets are reingested through coprophagy, which allows rabbits to eat green vegetation rapidly and get optimal nutrition from quick meals later in the safety of a protected location.

Recognized since 1992 as a separate species apart from the New England Cottontail (not shown) based on the size and shape of the skull and chromosomal differences. It is impossible to tell them apart in the field, so ranges are useful for identification in the areas where they both occur. The range of the Appalachian Cottontail extends in a band from northern Georgia up along the Appalachian Mountains to Pennsylvania. It occurs in Georgia only in the northern part of the state; New England Cottontails are not found anywhere in Georgia.

Eastern Cottontail
Sylvilagus floridanus

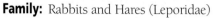

Family: Rabbits and Hares (Leporidae)

Size: L 14-18" (36-45 cm); T 1-2" (2.5-5 cm)

Weight: 2-4 lb. (.9-1.8 kg)

Description: Overall gray to light brown. Black-tipped hairs give it a grizzled appearance. Usually has a small white (rarely black) spot on forehead between the ears. Large pointed ears, rarely with a black outside edge. Distinctive rusty red nape. Brown tail with a white cotton-like underside.

Origin/Age: native; 1-3 years

Compare: More common than the Appalachian Cottontail (pg. 207), which lives only in parts of northern Georgia. The Marsh Rabbit (pg. 203) has shorter ears and is rusty red. Swamp Rabbit (pg. 215) is darker and found in the western half of the state.

Habitat: wide variety such as open fields, brush piles, rock piles, along rivers and streams, woodlands, thickets

Home: shallow nest, lined with soft plant material and fur, covered with dry grasses and leaves

Food: herbivore; grass, dandelions, other green plants in spring and summer; saplings, twigs, bark and other woody plants in winter

Sounds: loud high-pitched scream or squeal when caught by a predator such as a fox or coyote

Breeding: late Feb-Mar mating; 30 days gestation; starts to breed at 3 months

Young: 3-6 offspring up to 5 times per year; born naked and helpless with eyes closed

camouflaged

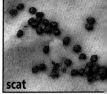

scat

Signs: small woody twigs and branches near the ground are cleanly cut off and at an angle, while browse from deer is higher up and has a ragged edge (due to the lack of upper incisors in deer), bark is stripped off of saplings and shrubs; dry, pea-sized light brown pellets, round and woody; soft green pellets are ingested and rarely seen

Activity: nocturnal, crepuscular; often very active during late winter and early spring when males fight to breed with females

Tracks: hind paw 3-4" (7.5-10 cm) long, forepaw 1" (2.5 cm) long, small and round; 1 set of 4 tracks; forepaws fall one in front of the other behind hind prints

Stan's Notes: The most widespread of the eight cottontail species in North America, seen in the eastern United States, all of Georgia and most of Mexico. Transplanted to many areas that historically did not have cottontails. Common name was given for its cotton ball-like tail.

Usually stays in a small area of only a couple acres. Often freezes, hunkers down and flattens ears if danger is near. Quickly runs in a zigzag pattern, circling back to its starting spot when flushed. Able to leap up to 12-15 feet (3.7-4.5 m) in a single bound while running. Also jumps sideways while running to break its scent trail. Uses a set of well-worn trails in winter, usually in thick cover of bushes. Cools itself on hot summer days by stretching out in shaded grassy areas.

Usually not a territorial animal, with fights among males breaking out only during mating season. Interspersed with chasing, males face each other, kick with front feet and jump high into the air.

After mating, the female excavates a small area for a nest, lines it with soft plants and fur from her chest for comfort and camou-flages the entrance. Mothers nurse their babies at dawn and dusk. Once the young open their eyes and are moving outside the nest, they are on their

cooling

own and get no further help from their mother. One of the most reproductively successful rabbit species in North America, with some females producing as many as 35 offspring annually; how-ever, most young do not live longer than 1 year.

Like other rabbits and hares, this species produces fecal pellets that are dry and brown or soft and green. Eats the green pellets to regain the nutrition that wasn't digested initially.

Swamp Rabbit
Sylvilagus acquaticus

Family: Rabbits and Hares (Leporidae)

Size: L 18-22" (45-56 cm); T 1-2" (2.5-5 cm)

Weight: 3½-5 lb. (1.6-2.3 kg)

Description: Short hair (pelage), overall dark brown, with the center of back darker than the sides. Gray underneath. Short broad ears, sparsely haired. Orange eye-ring. Feet and nape of neck rusty red. Brown tail with a white cotton-like underside.

Origin/Age: native; 1-3 years

Compare: Since cottontails are so similar, range can help identify. Swamp Rabbit is the largest cottontail and occurs mostly in the western half of Georgia. Marsh Rabbit (pg. 203) is seen in most parts of eastern, central and southern Georgia. Eastern Cottontail (pg. 211) lacks rusty red feet and is seen across Georgia. The Appalachian Cottontail (pg. 207) occurs in parts of northern Georgia.

Habitat: river bottoms, coastal marshes, just about any other place with standing water

Home: shallow nest, lined with soft plant material and fur, covered with dry grasses and leaves, under a fallen log, at the base of a tree

Food: herbivore; grass, other green plants

Sounds: loud high-pitched scream or squeal when caught by a predator such as a fox, coyote or raptor

Breeding: Jan-Sep mating; 38-40 days gestation; starts to breed during the first year

Young: 2-4 offspring 2-3 times per year; born furred, with eyes and ears closed, opening within days

215

Signs: small woody twigs and branches near the ground are cleanly cut off and at an angle; pea-sized, round, dry, woody, light brown pellets placed on logs and stumps or other high places

Activity: nocturnal, crepuscular; can also be seen during the day, often very active during February and March when males fight to breed with females

Tracks: hind paw 4-5" (10-13 cm) long, forepaw ½" (2.5 cm) long, small and round; 1 set of 4 tracks; forepaws fall one in front of the other behind hind prints

Stan's Notes: The smallest of the weasels. Solitary for most of the year, except for mating. Excellent sight, hearing and sense of smell. Can climb trees, but spends most of its time on the ground. Runs as fast as 6 mph (10 km/h) on flat ground. Often stands on hind legs to get a better look around.

winter

Fast, agile and small enough to follow its favorite food, the Meadow Vole (pg. 145), or mice into tunnels. Kills with a single bite to the base of the skull to sever the spinal cord. Can eat up to 40 percent of its own weight in food every day. Sometimes it kills more than it can eat and will cache the extra to consume later.

Like other weasels, it emits a strong pungent odor from glands near the base of its tail when excited or threatened. Also uses this scent to mark territory.

Male occupies a small territory of 2 acres (.8 ha). Territory of the female is even smaller. The male becomes sexually active at 8 months. The female matures at 4 months, but rarely breeds during the year of her birth.

Stan's Notes: Widespread across Georgia. An active predator that runs in a series of bounds with back arched and tail elevated. A good swimmer and will climb trees to pursue squirrels. Quickly locates prey using its excellent eyesight and sense of smell, dashes to grab it, then kills it with several bites to the base of the skull. Favorite foods include mice and voles. Sometimes hunts for larger prey such as rabbits. Eats its fill and caches the rest. Consumes 25-40 percent of its own body weight in food daily.

In Georgia and across the southern range, many individuals stay brown and do not turn white in winter.

winter

Uses scents and sounds to communicate with other weasels. Deposits scat on rocks and trails to mark territory. Both sexes apply an oily, odoriferous substance from their anal glands onto rocks, trees and other prominent landmarks to communicate territory, social status, sex and willingness to mate. The odor is rarely detectable by people, especially after a few days. Male territory is 25-55 acres (10-22 ha). Female territory is smaller. Defends territory against other weasels.

Solitary except during mating season and when a mother is with her young. Constructs nest in an abandoned animal burrow or beneath logs and rocks, using grass for nesting material along with the fur of small animals it has eaten.

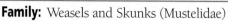

Mink
Mustela vison

Family: Weasels and Skunks (Mustelidae)

Size: L 14-20" (36-50 cm); T 6-8" (15-20 cm)

Weight: 1½-3½ lb. (.7-1.6 kg)

Description: Dark brown to nearly black or brown to blond, often with a luster. Same color belly and back. Small white patch on chin. Short, round dark ears. Long tubular body with short legs. A long bushy tail, darker near the tip. Male slightly larger than female.

Origin/Age: native; 5-10 years

Compare: Larger than the Long-tailed Weasel (pg. 223), which has lighter brown fur with a white-to-yellow underside.

Habitat: along rivers, lakes and streams, wetlands, farms, forests

Home: burrow, entrance is 4" (10 cm) wide

Food: carnivore; small to medium mammals such as voles, mice, chipmunks, rabbits and squirrels, but favors muskrats; also eats small birds, bird eggs, snakes, frogs, toads, crayfish and fish

Sounds: chatters, scolds, hisses, snarls when alarmed or fighting other minks

Breeding: Jan-Apr mating; 32-51 days gestation; implantation delayed, length of delay is dependent upon when the female mates during the season

Young: 3-6 offspring once per year; born covered with fine hair and eyes closed, eyes open at about 7 weeks, weaned at 8-9 weeks, mature at 5 months

brown morph

scat

Signs: small, thin dark scat, usually pointed at one end, usually containing bone, fur and fish scales, deposited on rocks and logs along lakes and rivers

Activity: nocturnal, diurnal; hunts for several hours, then rests several hours

Tracks: hind paw 2-3¼" (5-8 cm) long with 5 toes, forepaw 1¼-1¾" (3-4.5 cm) long with 5 toes, both round with well-defined nail marks; 1 set of 4 tracks when bounding; 12-25" (30-64 cm) stride; tracks may end at the edge of water

Stan's Notes: Also called American Mink. Often associated with water and seen along riverbanks and lakes in Georgia. Its thick, oily, waterproof fur provides great insulation and enables the animal to swim in nearly freezing water. Its partially webbed toes aid in swimming. Can swim underwater as far as 100 feet (30 m) before surfacing. Able to dive down to 15 feet (4.6 m) for one of its favorite foods, muskrats.

Hunts on land for chipmunks, rabbits, snakes and frogs. Moves in a series of loping bounds with its back arched and tail held out slightly above horizontal. When frightened or excited, releases an odorous substance from glands near the base of its tail.

Burrow is almost always near water, often under a tree root or in a riverbank. May use a hollow log or muskrat burrow after killing and eating the occupants. Active burrows will often have a strong odor near the entrance. Most burrows are temporary since minks are almost constantly on the move looking for their next meal.

The male maintains a territory of up to 40 acres (16 ha), with the female territory less than half the size. Will mark its territory by applying a pungent discharge on prominent rocks and logs. It is a polygamous breeder.

The pelt of a mink is considered to be one of the most luxurious. Demand for the fur has led to the establishment of mink ranches, where the fur color can be controlled by selective breeding.

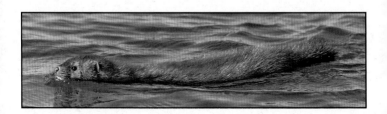

Northern River Otter
Lontra canadensis

Family: Weasels and Skunks (Mustelidae)

Size: L 2½-3½' (76-107 cm); T 11-20" (28-50 cm)

Weight: 10-30 lb. (4.5-13.5 kg)

Description: Overall dark brown-to-black fur, especially when wet, with a lighter brown-to-gray belly. Silver-to-gray chin and throat. Small ears and eyes. Short snout with white whiskers. Elongated body with a long thick tail, tapered at the tip. Male slightly larger than female.

Origin/Age: native; 7-20 years

Compare: Round-tailed Muskrat (pg. 153) and Muskrat (pg. 157) are much smaller and have long, thin naked tails. The American Beaver (pg. 165) has a wide flat tail. Mink (pg. 227) is much smaller and has a thinner tail.

Habitat: rivers, streams, medium to large lakes

Home: permanent and temporary dens

Food: carnivore, insectivore; fish, crayfish, frogs, small mammals, aquatic insects

Sounds: loud shrill cries when threatened, during play will grunt, growl and snort, chuckles when with mate or siblings

Breeding: Mar-Apr mating; 200-270 days gestation; implantation delayed for an unknown amount of time, entire reproduction process may take up to a year, female mates again days after giving birth

Young: 1-6 offspring once per year in March or April; born fully furred with eyes closed, eyes open at around 30 days, weaned at about 3 months

Signs: haul outs, slides and rolling areas; scat is dark brown to green, short segments frequently contain fish bones and scales or crayfish parts, deposited on lakeshores, riverbanks, rocks or logs in water

Activity: diurnal, nocturnal; active year-round, spends most of time in water, comes onto land to rest and sleep, curls up like a house cat to sleep

Tracks: hind paw 3½" (9 cm), forepaw slightly smaller, both round with a well-defined heel pad and toes spread evenly apart, 5 toes on all feet; 1 set of 4 tracks when bounding; 12-24" (30-61 cm) stride

Stan's Notes: Not a common skunk in Georgia, but widespread, with populations decreasing dramatically across the country. It is thought that the widespread use of insecticides is responsible for the decline, since one of the main foods of this species is insects.

Considered by some to have the finest, softest fur in the animal world. A semisocial animal, but secretive. Fast, agile and adept at climbing trees. An expert mouser that, like a house cat, is good at controlling small mammal and insect populations around farms. Constantly on the move, looking for its next meal. Much more carnivorous than the Striped Skunk (pg. 239).

Also called Civet Cat, but this is a misleading name because it is neither a civet (mongoose, member of the Viverridae family), nor is it a cat. Species name *putorius* is Latin and refers to the pungent smell of its spray.

When threatened, it rushes forward, stomps its feet and stands on its forepaws with hind end elevated. Agile enough to spray from this position. Can spray up to 10 feet (3 m) with surprising accuracy. Odor is similar to that of the Striped Skunk.

Female matures sexually at 9-11 months. Mother raises the young without any help from the male.

Striped Skunk
Mephitis mephitis

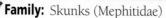

Family: Skunks (Mephitidae)

Size: L 20-24" (50-61 cm); T 7-14" (18-36 cm)

Weight: 6-12 lb. (2.7-5.4 kg)

Description: Variable stripe patterns. Black with a large white stripe from ears to tail, sometimes splitting down the hind quarters. Large bushy tail, shorter or equal to body length, white or black with white sides. Thin white stripe down the center of head between ears and eyes. Male larger than female.

Origin/Age: native; 2-5 years

Compare: The Eastern Spotted Skunk (pg. 235) is much smaller, has spots, more stripes and is much less common.

Habitat: woodlands, river bottoms, farmlands, woodland edges, prairies, fields, suburban and urban areas

Home: burrow, often in hollow log or tree crevice, under a deck, porch, firewood or rock pile in summer

Food: omnivore; insects, spiders, small mammals, earthworms, grubs, bird eggs, amphibians, corn, fruit, berries, nuts, seeds, reptiles

Sounds: generally quiet; will stomp front feet and exhale in a loud "pfittt," also chatters its teeth

Breeding: Feb-Apr mating; 62-66 days gestation; implantation delayed until 18-20 days after mating

Young: 4-7 offspring once per year; born naked with black and white skin (matching the color of its future fur coat) and eyes closed, musky odor at 8-10 days, eyes open at about 24 days

babies in burrow   juvenile

Signs: pungent odor, more obvious when the skunk has sprayed, can be detected even when it has not sprayed; segmented cylindrical scat, often dark, deposited on trails and at entrance to the den

scat

Activity: mostly nocturnal; more active during summer than winter

Tracks: hind paw 2-3½" (5-9 cm) long with 5 toes and a well-defined heel pad, looking flat-footed, forepaw 1-1¾" (2.5-4.5 cm) long and wide with 5 toes; alternating fore and hind prints are very close together when walking, 4-6" (10-15 cm) stride

Stan's Notes: Member of an order of animals with unique backbone joints that allow more bending than is possible in animals without the special joints. Animals in this group are found only in South, Central and North America. There are several armadillo species, but only the Nine-banded occurs in North America. It is expanding its range in the United States, having moved up from Mexico.

Historically, several armadillo species populated Georgia millions of years ago. The current armadillos are a combination of a wild population moving eastward from Texas and captive individuals that escaped during the 1920-30s.

Gets the common name "Nine" from the number of armored, jointed (articulated) plates on its body. Able to curl up into a tight ball, with the plate on top of its head protecting the joint where the front and back of the armored shell meet. When threatened, the first defense of an armadillo is to run off or hide in its burrow, where it lodges itself, using its armor as protection. Armored up inside a burrow makes it nearly impossible to pull the animal out. If the burrow is not near, it will roll up into an impenetrable ball.

Eyesight is not that great, so sometimes it stands upright to sniff the air for danger, supporting itself with its tail. Spends most of its time out of the burrow with its nose to the ground, sniffing for insects or other food. An excellent excavator, digging under fallen logs or tearing apart logs, using its short, thick, powerful legs and long toe nails to burrow and search out food. A desirable animal to have around due to the large number of insects it consumes at ranches and farms.

Young can walk within hours of birth. Appearing like miniature piglets, they follow their mother around in a line, single file.

Virginia Opossum
Didelphis virginiana

Family: Opossums (Didelphidae)

Size: L 25-30" (64-76 cm); T 10-20" (25-50 cm)

Weight: 4-14 lb. (1.8-6.3 kg)

Description: Gray-to-brown body, occasionally nearly black. A white head, throat and belly. Long narrow snout with a pink nose. Wide mouth. Oval, naked black ears. Long, scaly, naked, semiprehensile pinkish tail. Short legs. Five pink toes on feet. First toe on each hind foot is thumb-like and lacks a nail.

Origin/Age: native; 3-5 years

Compare: Round-tailed Muskrat (pg. 153) and Muskrat (pg. 157) are much smaller, all brown and rarely far from water. Norway Rat (pg. 129) shares the long naked tail, but is smaller, lacks a pink nose and the large dark ears and is rarely seen in trees.

Habitat: deciduous forests, farmlands, yards, grasslands, wetlands, along streams and rivers, cities

Home: leaf nest in an underground den or hollow log

Food: omnivore; insects, sunflower and thistle seeds, nuts, berries, fruit, leaves, bird eggs, fish, reptiles, amphibians, small mammals, road kill, worms

Sounds: low growls, hisses and shows teeth if threatened, soft clicks between mothers and young

Breeding: Jan-Feb mating; 8-14 days gestation

Young: 2-13 (usually 5-6) offspring once per year; newborns the size of a navy bean crawl to mother's external fur-lined pouch, where they attach to a nipple for as long as 2 months

247

in pouch

scat

Signs: overturned garbage cans; scat on ground under sunflower seed and Nyjer thistle feeders

Activity: nocturnal; can be seen during the day in winter

Tracks: hind paw 2" (5 cm) long with 5 toes, large thumb-like first toe points inward and lacks a nail, forepaw 1½" (4 cm) long with 5 toes spread out; fore and hind prints are parallel, 7" (18 cm) stride, often has a tail drag mark

Stan's Notes: Raccoons are native only to the Americas from Central America to the United States and lower Canada. Northern Raccoon is found across Georgia in nearly all habitats. Common name is from the Algonquian Indian word *arougbcoune*, meaning "he scratches with his hands." Known for the ability to open such objects as doors, coolers and latches. Uses its nimble fingers to feel around the edges of ponds, rivers and lakes for crayfish and frogs.

Known to occasionally wash its food before eating, hence the species name *lotor*, meaning "washer." However, it is not washing its food, but kneading and tearing it apart. The water helps it feel the parts that are edible and those that are not. A strong swimmer.

Able to climb any tree very quickly and can come down headfirst or tail end first. Its nails can grip bark no matter which way it climbs because it can rotate its hind feet nearly 180 degrees so that the hind toes always point up the tree.

Active at night, sleeping in hollow trees or other dens during the day. Often mistakenly associated with forests. Also lives in grasslands, using underground dens, but never is far from water.

Usually solitary as an adult. Does not hibernate but may sleep or simply hole up in a comfortable den in January and February, depending on the weather. Will occasionally den in small groups of the same sex, usually males, or females without young.

Males wander many miles in search of a mate. Females use the same den for several months while raising their young, but move out afterward and find a new place to sleep each night. Males are not involved in raising young. Young remain with the adult female for nearly a year.

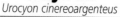

Gray Fox
Urocyon cinereoargenteus

Family: Wolves, Foxes and Coyote (Canidae)

Size: L 22-24" (56-61 cm); T 10-17" (25-43 cm); H 14-15" (36-38 cm)

Weight: 7-13 lb. (3.2-5.9 kg)

Description: Grizzled gray fox with a rust red nape, shoulders and rust red across the chest. Large pointed ears, trimmed in white. White chin, neck and belly. Large bushy tail with a black tip and ridge of stiff dark hairs along the top.

Origin/Age: native; 5-10 years

Compare: The Red Fox (pg. 259) has a white-tipped tail. Coyote (pg. 263) shares the grayish appearance and black-tipped tail, but is larger than the Gray Fox and has longer legs.

Habitat: deciduous forests, pine forests, river valleys, brushy areas, suburban and urban areas

Home: den, mostly in a natural cavity such as a log or a crevice in rock, will enlarge a prairie dog burrow, unlike a Red Fox den, the den of a Gray Fox lacks a mound of dirt in front of the entrance

Food: omnivore; small mammals such as mice, moles, voles, rabbits and hares; also eats berries, apples, nuts, fish, insects and carrion

Sounds: hoarse high-pitched barks, yelps to steady high-pitched screams, mournful cries; much less vocal than the Red Fox

Breeding: winter (Jan-Mar) mating; 51-53 days gestation

Young: 1-7 kits once per year in April or May; born helpless with black fur and eyes closed

Signs: urine and piles of feces, mostly on conspicuous landmarks such as a prominent rock, stump or trail; cylindrical scat with a tapered end, can be very dark if berries were eaten, often contains hair and bones

Activity: mostly nocturnal, crepuscular; can be seen during the day in winter, especially when overcast

Tracks: forepaw 1½" (4 cm) long, oval, hind paw slightly smaller; straight line of single tracks; hind paws fall near or directly onto fore prints (direct register) when walking, often obliterating the forepaw tracks, 10-14" (25-36 cm) stride when walking

Stan's Notes: Common throughout Georgia. Dens in woodpiles, hollow dead trees, culverts and underneath fallen trees and buildings.

The scientific name provides a very good description of this animal. The genus *Urocyon* is Greek for "tailed dog." The species *cinereoargenteus* is Latin and means "silver" or "gray and black."

Also called Treefox because it often climbs trees. Climbs to escape larger predators more than it does to find food. Sometimes it will rest in a tree. Shinnies up, pivoting its front legs at the shoulder joints to grab the trunk and pushes with hind feet. Able to rotate its front legs more than other canids. Once up the trunk, it jumps from branch to branch and has been seen up to 20 feet (6.1 m) high. Descends by backing down or running headfirst down a sloping branch.

Thought to mate for life. Male often travels 50 miles (81 km) to establish territory. A pair will defend a territory of 2-3 square miles (5-8 sq. km).

The kits are weaned at about six weeks. Male doesn't enter the den, but helps feed the family by bringing in food. Young disperse at the end of summer just before the parents start mating again.

Red Fox
Vulpes vulpes

Family: Wolves, Foxes and Coyote (Canidae)

Size: L 22-24" (56-61 cm); T 13-17" (33-43 cm); H 15-16" (38-40 cm)

Weight: 7-15 lb. (3.2-6.8 kg)

Description: Usually rusty red with dark highlights, but can vary from light yellow to black. Large pointed ears trimmed in black with white inside. White jowls, chest and belly. Legs nearly black. Large bushy tail with a white tip. Fluffy coat in winter and spring. Molts by June, appearing smaller and thinner.

Origin/Age: native; 5-10 years

Compare: Gray Fox (pg. 255) is not as red and has a black-tipped tail. Smaller than the Coyote (pg. 263), usually more red and has a white-tipped tail. All other wild canids lack a tail with a white tip.

Habitat: woodlands, rangelands, grasslands, prairies, pine forests, deciduous forests, suburbs, cities

Home: den, sometimes a hollow log, may dig a den under a log or a rock in a bank of a stream or in a hillside created when land was cut to build a road, often has a mound of dirt up to 3' (.9 m) high in front of the main entrance with scat deposits

Food: omnivore; small mammals such as mice, moles, voles, rabbits and hares; also eats berries, apples, nuts, fish, insects and carrion

Sounds: hoarse high-pitched barks, yelps to steady high-pitched screams, mournful cries

Breeding: winter (Jan-Mar) mating; 51-53 days gestation

Young: 1-10 kits once per year in April or May

summer coat

winter coat

silver morph | dark morph

scat

Signs: cylindrical scat with a tapered end, can be very dark if berries were eaten, frequently contains hair and bones, often found on a trail, prominent rock or stump or at den entrance

Activity: mainly nocturnal, crepuscular; rests during the middle of the night

Tracks: forepaw 2" (5 cm) long, oval, with hind paw slightly smaller; straight line of single tracks; hind paws fall near or directly onto fore prints (direct register) when walking, often obliterating the forepaw tracks, 10-14" (25-36 cm) stride when walking

Stan's Notes: This is the most widely distributed wild canid in the world, ranging across North America, Europe, Asia and northern Africa. Some European Red Foxes were introduced into North America in the 1790s, resulting in confusion about the original distribution and lineage.

Usually alone. Very smart, learning from experience. Pounces onto prey like a cat. Between hunting trips, curls into a ball and sleeps at the base of a tree or rock.

Hunts for mice, moles and other small prey by stalking, looking and listening. Hearing differs from the other mammals.

den entrance

Hears low-frequency sounds, enabling it to detect small animals digging and gnawing underground. Chases larger prey such as rabbits and squirrels. Hunts even when full, caching extra food underground. Finds cached food by memory and smell.

Mated pairs actively defend their territory from other foxes, but they are often killed by coyotes or wolves. Uses a den only several weeks for birthing and raising young. Parents bring food to kits in the den. At first, parents regurgitate food. Later they bring in fresh meat and live prey for their young to practice killing. Uses 3-4 dens simultaneously. Moves kits from den to den so they are not all in the same place at the same time. Young are dispersed at the end of their first summer, with males (dog foxes) traveling 100-150 miles (161-242 km)–much farther than the females (vixens)–to establish their own territories.

kits

Coyote
Canis latrans

Family: Wolves, Foxes and Coyote (Canidae)

Size: L 3-3½' (.9-1.1 m); T 12-15" (30-38 cm); H 18-24" (45-61 cm)

Weight: 20-40 lb. (9-18 kg)

Description: Tan fur with black and orange highlights. Large, pointed reddish orange ears with white interior. Long narrow snout with a white upper lip. Long legs and bushy black-tipped tail.

Origin/Age: native; 5-10 years

Compare: Smaller than the Red Wolf (pg. 267), with larger ears and a narrower pointed snout. The Red Fox (pg. 259) has black legs and a white-tipped tail.

Habitat: all habitats, rural, suburban and urban areas, forests, fields, farms

Home: den, usually in a riverbank, hillside, under a rock or tree root, entrance 12-24" (30-61 cm) high, can be up to 30' (9.1 m) deep and ends in small chamber where female gives birth; female may dig own den or enlarge a fox or badger den

Food: omnivore; small mammals, reptiles, amphibians, birds, bird eggs, insects, fruit, carrion

Sounds: barks like a dog, calls to others result in a chorus of high-pitched howling and yipping; sounds different from the lower, deeper call of the Red Wolf, which rarely yips

Breeding: mid to late winter; 63 days average gestation

Young: 4-6 pups once per year in April or May; born with eyes closed

summer coat

Signs: cylindrical scat (shape is similar to that of domestic dog excrement), often containing fur and bones, along well-worn game trails, on prominent rocks and at trail intersections

scat

Activity: nocturnal, crepuscular, diurnal; can be seen for several hours after sunrise and before sunset

Tracks: forepaw 2¼ (5.5 cm) long, round to slightly oval, hind paw slightly smaller; straight line of single tracks; hind paws fall near or directly onto fore prints (direct register) when walking, often obliterating the forepaw tracks, 12-15" (30-38 cm) stride when walking, 24-30" (61-76 cm) stride when running

Stan's Notes: Sometimes called Brush Wolf or Prairie Wolf, even though this animal is obviously not a wolf. The genus name *Canis* is Latin for "dog." The species name *latrans* is also Latin and means "barking." It is believed that the common name "Coyote" comes from the Aztec word *coyotl*, which means "barking dog."

Not seen east of the Mississippi River until the 1950s; now occurs in every state. Found throughout Georgia. Often viewed as a gluttonous outlaw, although it is only guilty of surviving a rapidly changing environment and outright slaughter by people. Intelligent and playful, much like the domestic dog. Hunts alone or in small groups. Uses its large ears to hear small mammals beneath vegetation.

Most coyotes run with their tails down unlike dogs and wolves, which run with their tails level to upright. A fast runner, it can travel 25-30 mph (40-48 km/h). May reach 40 mph (64 km/h) for short distances. Some coyotes tracked with radio collars are known to travel more than 400 miles (644 km) over several days.

Usually courts for 2-3 months before breeding. A monogamous animal, with mated pairs staying together for many years or for life.

Pups emerge from the den at 2-3 weeks and are weaned at 5-7 weeks. Mother will move her pups from the den when she feels threatened. Mother often gets help raising young from other group members and her mate. Pups do not return to the den once they are able to survive on their own. Mother abandons the den once the pups leave and will often return year after year in spring to use the same den.

EXTIRPATED
no longer found

FORMER RANGE

Red Wolf
Canis rufus

Family: Wolves, Foxes and Coyote (Canidae)

Size: L 4-4½' (1.2-1.4 m); T 14-17" (36-43 cm); H 24-36" (61-91 cm)

Weight: 40-80 lb. (18-36 kg)

Description: Usually gray with dark highlights. Reddish tinge, especially on upper legs and face. Large bushy tail, black-tipped. Long pointed ears, widely spaced, with rusty backs. Narrow muzzle and large nose pad. Wide band of white around lips. Long legs and large feet. Male is slightly larger than female.

Origin/Age: native; 5-15 years

Compare: Coyote (pg. 263) is smaller, has shorter legs and a narrow white lip mark. Red Wolf has a wider space between its ears and usually holds its tail straight out when traveling, while Coyote holds its tail downward.

Habitat: forests, brushlands, grasslands, coastal prairies

Home: shelter or den only for raising young, den can be 5-15' (1.5-4.6 m) deep, frequently more than 1 entrance, fan of dirt at entrance, often scattered bones and fur laying about; used for many years

Food: omnivore; mice, rabbits, hares, deer and bears; also eats berries, grass, insects and fish

Sounds: barks and howls, low deep howling may rise and fall in pitch or remain the same; rarely has a series of yips or yelps at the end, like the Coyote

Breeding: Jan-Feb mating; 63-65 days gestation

Young: 2-5 pups once a year; born helpless, eyes closed

267

Signs: scrapes in the dirt, urine on posts, rocks and stumps; scat looks like the excrement of a domestic dog, but it is larger and contains hairs and bone fragments

Activity: nocturnal, more diurnal in winter

Tracks: forepaw 5½-6½" (14-16 cm) long, hind paw slightly smaller, both round with clear claw marks; straight line of single tracks; hind paws fall near or directly onto fore prints (direct register) when walking, often obliterating the forepaw tracks, 15-30" (38-76 cm) stride; rarely walks along roads like a domestic dog

Stan's Notes: Once ranged from Illinois to eastern Texas, east to Florida, and up through Georgia and the coast to New England. Eliminated from Georgia in the early 1900s due to changes in land use over the years and persecution by people. During the 1970s, the last of the remaining 17 Red Wolves were taken into captivity to start a breeding program. Efforts are now underway to reestablish a population in the wild.

With so many coyotes in Georgia, it is likely that the larger wild dog-like sightings might actually be coyotes. It is believed that the success of the coyote is due to it filling the niche that the Red Wolf had once occupied.

The entire wild population of Red Wolf, nearly 100 individuals, is in North Carolina. Reintroduction into North Carolina began in the late 1980s along the Great Smoky Mountains. A small population is kept in captivity for reintroduction purposes.

Like other wolf species, the Red Wolf travels great distances in its territory. Consumes 2-5 pounds (.9-2.3 kg) of meat per day, but can go for weeks without food. Feeds mainly on small mammals such as rabbits, rats, mice, raccoons and birds.

Runs in small packs consisting of family members. Packs have a well-defined hierarchy, with one male leader, called alpha, and his female mate, also alpha. Young are subordinate to adults and make up the rest of the pack. Young Red Wolves of the previous year do not help raise the young of the new year.

Bobcat
Lynx rufus

Family: Cats (Felidae)

Size: L 2¼-3½' (69-107 cm); T 3-7" (7.5-18 cm); H 18-24" (45-61 cm)

Weight: 14-30 lb. (6.3-13.5 kg)

Description: Tawny brown during summer. Light gray during winter with dark streaks and spots. Long stiff fur projects down from jowls and tapers to a point (cheek ruffs). Triangular ears, tipped with short black hairs (tufts). Prominent white spot on the back of ears. Dark horizontal barring on upper legs. Short stubby tail with a black tip on the top and sides and a white underside. Male slightly larger than female.

Origin/Age: native; 10-15 years

Compare: Much smaller than the Cougar (pg. 275), which has a long rope-like tail. Look for ear tufts and a white underside of tail to help identify Bobcat.

Habitat: wide variety, mixed forests, fields, farmlands, suburban areas, cities

Home: den, often in a hollow log, rock crevice or under a pile of tree branches filled with leaves

Food: carnivore; medium to small mammals such as rabbits and mice; also eats birds and carrion

Sounds: raspy meows and yelps, purrs when content

Breeding: Feb-Mar mating; 60-70 days gestation

Young: 1-7 (usually 3) kittens once per year in April or May

mother and young

scat

Signs: scratching posts with claw marks 3-4' (.9-1.2 m) aboveground, caches of larger kills covered with a light layer of leaves and twigs, scent posts marked with urine; long cylindrical scat, contains hair and bones, often buried, sometimes visible beneath a thin layer of dirt and debris

Activity: nocturnal, diurnal; often rests on hot days in a sheltered spot such as under a fallen log or in a rock crevice

Tracks: forepaw and hind paw 2" (5 cm), round, multi-lobed heel pad, 4 toes on all feet, lacking claw marks; straight line of tracks; hind paws fall near or on fore prints (direct register) when walking, often obliterating forepaw tracks, 9-13" (23-33 cm) stride

Stan's Notes: This is the most common wildcat species in the country and Georgia. Thrives in nearly all habitat types, even on coastal islands. The common name refers to the short, stubby or "bobbed" tail. Frequently walks with tail curled upward, which exposes the white underside, making this animal easy to identify. Makes sounds similar to a house cat.

Often uses the same trails in its territory to patrol for rabbits, which is its favorite food, and other prey. Does not climb trees as much as the Cougar (pg. 275), but swims well. Hunts by stalking or laying in wait to attack (ambushing). Ambushes prey by rushing forward, chases and captures it, then kills it with a bite to the neck. Has been known to go without eating for several weeks during periods of famine.

Male has a larger territory than female. Usually solitary except for mating and when mothers are with young. Male will seek out a female in heat. Several males may follow a female until she is ready for mating.

Female does not breed until her second year. She has a primary (natal) den in which kittens are born and live for a short time after birth. Female also has secondary dens in her territory, where she may move her young if the natal den is disturbed. Dens are used only by the females and young. Mother raises young on her own.

kittens

Kittens are born well furred and with spots. Their eyes are closed at birth and open at about 10 days. They are weaned at approximately 8 weeks, when they start to hunt with their mother. Young stay with their mother until about 7 months, when she disperses them to mate.

Cougar
Puma concolor

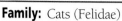

Family: Cats (Felidae)

Size: L 5-6' (1.5-1.8 m); T 24-36" (61-91 cm); H 30-36" (76-91 cm)

Weight: M 80-267 lb. (36-120 kg); F 64-142 lb. (29-64 kg)

Description: Overall light to tawny brown with light gray-to-white underside. White upper lip and chin, pink nose, dark spot at base of white whiskers. Small oval ears. Long legs. Large round feet. Long rope-like tail with a dark tip.

Origin/Age: native; 10-20 years

Compare: Bobcat (pg. 271) is much smaller, with a short tail. Look for a long rope-like tail to help identify the Cougar.

Habitat: river valleys, woodlands, unpopulated locations

Home: den, often a sheltered rock crevice, thicket, cave or other protected place; female uses den only to give birth, male does not use den

Food: carnivore; larger mammals such as rabbits, deer, opossums, raccoons and skunks

Sounds: purrs when content or with cubs, growls, snarls and hisses when threatened or in defense, loud frightening scream during mating, rarely roars

Breeding: year-round mating; 90-100 days gestation

Young: 1-6 (usually 3) cubs every 2 years; born helpless and blind, covered with dark spots until 3 months, leaves den at 40-70 days and does not return, remains with mother until 15 months

275

cubs

scat

Signs: long scratches and gashes above 5' (1.5 m) on larger tree trunks, small piles of urine-soaked dirt and debris (serving as scent posts), caches of uneaten prey covered with small branches and leaves; large cylindrical scat up to 10" (25 cm) long and 2" (5 cm) wide, contains hair and bones, sometimes lightly covered with dirt

Activity: primarily nocturnal, to a lesser extent crepuscular; active all year, usually rests in a tree in daytime, rests near a recent kill

Tracks: forepaw and hind paw 5-6" (13-15 cm), round, lobed heel pad, toes evenly spread, lacks claw marks; straight line of tracks; hind paws fall near or onto fore prints (direct register) when walking, often obliterating forepaw tracks, 12-28" (30-71 cm) stride

Stan's Notes: The Cougar was the most widely ranging cat in the New World in the early 1800s, from Canada to the tip of South America. It was hunted by government professionals to protect livestock from attack until the 1960s. Now seen in Georgia only in scattered remote, unpopulated areas. Often secretive and avoids humans, but has been known to attack people.

Contrary to the popular belief that it harms the deer population, it usually hunts and kills only about once each week, feeding for many days on the same kill. It hunts by stalking and springing from cover or dropping from a tree. Frequently drags its kill to a secluded area to eat, buries the carcass and returns to feed over the next couple days, often at night. It is an excellent climber and can leap distances up to 20 feet (6.1 m). Will swim if necessary.

Some people mistakenly think this cat will make a good pet and do not know what to do when their "pet" starts to knock down family members and bite them. These "pets" are released and then often turn up in suburban areas. Usually these are the animals that attack people since they have lost their fear of humans.

Home range of the male is 54-115 square miles (140-299 sq. km) and excludes other male cougars. Female range is nearly half the size of the male territory.

Solitary animal except for females with cubs and when mating. During that time the male travels and sleeps with the female for up to a couple weeks. The female matures sexually at 2-3 years of age. Only the females raise the young.

Wild Hog
Sus scrofa

Family: Old World Swine (Suidae)

Size: L 4-6' (1.2-1.8 m); T 6-12" (15-30 cm); H 2-3' (61-91 cm)

Weight: M 200-400 lb. (90-180 kg); F 75-300 lb. (34-135 kg)

Description: Extremely variable in color from dark brown and black to gray and white. Large thick body, long pointed snout and short dark legs. Thick fur and well-furred ears. Tail is furred and hangs straight down. Tusks up to 9" (23 cm) long, curling out alongside of mouth. Tiny dark eyes. Female has the same colors, but is smaller and lacks tusks.

Origin/Age: non-native; 15-20 years

Compare: No other pig-like animal occurs in the wilds of Georgia.

Habitat: open forests, ranches, farms

Home: no den or nest, rests out in the open or in open forests; female does not seek shelter to give birth, but makes a bed for birthing not far from water

Food: omnivore; grasses and other green plants, insects, mammals, reptiles, amphibians, birds

Sounds: snorts and grunts similar to domestic pigs

Breeding: year-round mating; 16 weeks gestation

Young: 5-7 piglets twice per year; only 6-8" (15-20 cm) at birth, usually brown with pale longitudinal body stripes, able to walk and follow mother at 1 week, nurses for 3 months

279

Signs: large holes in the ground where plants, crops, fences, posts or other objects were uprooted, mud wallowing holes; mass of pellets or tubular segments, usually near uprooted plants

Activity: diurnal, nocturnal, crepuscular; feeds for up to several hours, sits down to rest for up to 2 hours, then feeds again

Tracks: front hoof 2½-3" (6-7.5 cm) long, hind hoof slightly smaller, widely split at the front with a point in front; neat line of paired tracks, slightly offset; hind hooves fall near fore prints (no direct register) when walking

Stan's Notes: Spanish explorer Hernando de Soto brought pigs to the United States in 1539. Most Wild Hogs seen today are descendants of the European wild hogs that were introduced into the United States for food or sporting purposes. Some are the progeny of escaped domestic swine that became feral over just two generations. Wild and domestic hogs interbreed, producing traits of both species such as a cartilaginous, flexible snout. Now found in over half of the United States, mainly in the South, with range expanding northward.

Wild Hogs prefer forests that produce acorn crops. In the absence of this, they will live in open woodlands and other areas not far from water. Their presence has a noticeable impact on native wildlife and plant life, as well as on crops and livestock, and, for this reason, the animals are not welcome in many places. Other areas, however, embrace their presence with managed hunting. By pushing out native species, they represent one of the most serious conservation threats.

Also called Feral Pig, Wild Boar, Russian Wild Boar and Razorback. A female (sow) and her young (piglets) will feed together and sometimes join other groups in herds of up to 35 individuals. The male (boar) tends to be solitary unless it is breeding season. Boars will fight, using their tusks to determine dominance and the right to breed.

Piglets stay with their mother for a year. They are usually brown with pale longitudinal body stripes at birth, and become sexually mature at just 18 months of age.

male

Fallow Deer
Dama dama

Family: Deer (Cervidae)

Size: L 4½-5½' (1.4-1.7 m); T 8-15" (20-38 cm); H 3-3½' (.9-1.1 m)

Weight: M 175-225 lb. (79-101 kg); F 75-100 lb. (34-45 kg)

Description: Highly variable, with several forms. Rusty red to tan with white spots on back and sides merging into a line. May have a narrow black stripe along the back. White belly and legs. Small head and ears. Male has large, broad flattened (palmate) antlers with many tines; young males have spike antlers. Male gets darker and spots fade during winter. Female is smaller and lacks antlers. Both sexes have a prominent larynx (Adam's apple).

Origin/Age: non-native; 5-15 years

Compare: White-tailed Deer (pg. 287) lacks the broad flat antlers of the male Fallow Deer. Look for the Adam's apple to help identify Fallow Deer.

Habitat: grasslands, open meadows, ranches

Home: no den or nest; sleeps in a different spot every night, beds may be concentrated in one area, does not use a shelter in bad weather or winter

Food: herbivore; grasses, other green plants in summer, browse in winter includes oak and hackberry

Sounds: male gives a deep bellow and belching during rut, female bleats

Breeding: Sep-Nov mating; 7-8 months gestation

Young: 1 fawn (sometimes 2) once per year in May or June; walks within hours of birth

283

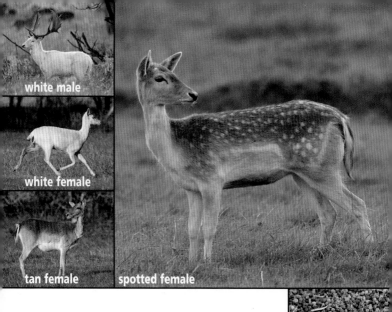

white male

white female

tan female

spotted female

scat

Signs: grass or other green plants cut off low to the ground, beds or flattened areas in the grass indicating resting or sleeping, often under trees

Activity: nocturnal, crepuscular; most active in early morning and again at the end of daylight

Tracks: front hoof 2½-3½" (6-9 cm) long, hind hoof slightly smaller, both with a split heart shape with the point in the front; neat line of single tracks; hind hooves fall near or directly onto fore prints (direct register) when walking

Stan's Notes: A handsome medium-sized deer, highly variable in color, with several color morphs in Georgia: rust, tan, white and black, the most common being rust with spots. Darker varieties usually hide the spots and stripes. Various color morphs can be seen in one herd. Both sexes are lighter colored in summer and darker during winter. The darker winter coat often diminishes or hides the white spots.

The Fallow Deer has a long association with people, dating back to before recorded history. The Romans introduced it to central Europe and it was further introduced from Europe and Asia. It is the most widely kept deer all over the world for hunting as food. Many escaped into the wild and are thriving. In Georgia many individuals are kept on private ranches for hunting purposes, and several small herds occur in the wild. Often tame and kept as semi-domesticated animals in parks and zoos.

The genus and species name *Dama* is Latin and used for roe deer, gazelles and antelopes. Adult males (bucks) display a moose-like flattened (palmate) antler. Only bucks have antlers, with young males growing and casting thin narrow antlers each season. After 3-4 years of age the males start to grow flattened (palmate) antlers with many small tines. These antlers become very large at about ages 6-7 and look out of place compared with the body. The antlers start to decline in size from this point on.

male

White-tailed Deer
Odocoileus virginianus

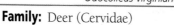

Family: Deer (Cervidae)

Size: L 4-7' (1.2-2.1 m); T 6-12" (15-30 cm); H 3-4' (.9- 1.2 m)

Weight: M 100-300 lb. (45-135 kg); F 75-200 lb. (34-90 kg)

Description: Reddish brown during summer, grayish brown during winter. Large ears, white inside with black edges. A white eye-ring, nose band, chin, throat and belly. Brown tail with a black tip and white underside. Male antlers have many small tines originating from a central beam; antler spread is 12-24" (30-61 cm). Female is overall smaller, has a thinner neck and lacks antlers.

Origin/Age: native; 5-10 years

Compare: Fallow Deer (pg. 283) has white spots, and the male Fallow has distinctive flattened antlers.

Habitat: many habitats such as woodlands, ranchlands, wetlands and scrublands

Home: no den or nest; sleeps in a different spot every night, beds may be concentrated in one area, does not use a shelter in bad weather

Food: herbivore; grasses and other green plants, acorns and nuts in summer, twigs and buds in winter

Sounds: loud whistle-like snorts, male grunts, fawn bleats

Breeding: Oct-Dec mating; 6-7 months gestation

Young: 1-2 fawns once per year from April through June; rare to have 3-4; covered with white spots, walks within hours of birth

young male

tree rub female

Signs: browsed twigs that are ripped or torn (due to the lack of upper incisor teeth), tree rubs (saplings scraped or stripped of bark) made by male while polishing antlers during the rut, oval depressions in grass or leaves are evidence of beds; round, hard brown pellets during winter, segmented cylindrical masses of scat in spring and summer

scat

Activity: nocturnal, crepuscular; moves along same trails to visit feeding areas, most active in early morning and the end of day

Tracks: front hoof 2-3" (5-7.5 cm) long, hind hoof slightly smaller, both with a split heart shape with the point in the front; neat line of single tracks; hind hooves fall near or directly onto fore prints (direct register) when walking

Stan's Notes: A common and widespread mammal in Georgia, adapting well to suburban environments.

fawn

In summer, antlers are covered with a furry skin known as velvet. Velvet contains a network of blood vessels that supplies nutrients to growing antlers. New antler growth begins after the male (buck) drops his antlers in January or February. Some females (does) grow antlers. Antler growth is tied to available nutrition. It is impossible to judge the age of a buck by the number of antler tines or antler size due to the direct correlation between antlers and nutrition. Examining teeth is a better way to estimate age.

Grows longer guard hairs in winter, giving the deer an overall gray color and larger appearance than in summer. Hairs of the winter coat are thick, hollow and provide excellent insulation.

Usually restricts its movement to a relatively small home range and is dependent on the location of the food supply. Eats 5-9 pounds (2.3-4.1 kg) of food per day, preferring acorns in fall and fresh grass and other green leaves in spring. Research shows that Whitetails eat up to 500 different plants. The four-chambered stomach enables the deer to get nutrients from poor food sources, such as twigs, and eat and drink substances that are unsuitable for people, including poison ivy and deadly mushrooms.

Able to run up to 37 mph (60 km/h), jump up to 8½ feet (2.6 m) high and leap 30 feet (9.1 m). Also an excellent swimmer.

For two weeks after their birth, fawns lay still all day long while their mother is away feeding. These babies are not abandoned; the mother nurses them during the evening and at night.

Black Bear
Ursus americanus

Family: Bears (Ursidae)

Size: L 4½-6' (1.4-1.8 m); T 3-7" (7.5-18 cm); H 3-3½' (.9-1.1 m)

Weight: M 100-900 lb. (45-405 kg); F 90-525 lb. (41-236 kg)

Description: Nearly all black, sometimes brown, tan or cinnamon. Short round ears. Light brown snout. May have a small white patch on its chest. Short tail, which often goes unnoticed.

Origin/Age: native; 15-30 years

Compare: The only bear species in Georgia.

Habitat: all forest types, grasslands

Home: den, underneath a fallen tree or in a rock crevice or cave, may dig a den 5-6' (1.5-1.8 m) deep with a small cavity at the end; male sometimes hibernates on the ground without shelter

Food: omnivore; leaves, nuts, roots, fruit, berries, grass, insects, fish, small mammals, carrion

Sounds: huffs, puffs or grunts and groans when walking, loud snorts made by air forced from nostrils, loud roars when fighting and occasionally when mating, motor-like humming when content

Breeding: Jun-Jul mating; 60-90 days gestation; implantation delayed until November after mating

Young: 1-5 (usually 2) cubs every other year in January or February; born covered with fine dark fur, weighing only ½-1 lb. (.2-.5 kg)

claw marks | brown morph

scat

Signs: series of long narrow scars on tree trunks, usually as high as the bear can reach, made by scratching and biting, rub marks with snagged hair on the lower part of tree trunks or on large rocks, made by rubbing and scratching when shedding its winter coat; large dark cylindrical scat or piles of loose scat, usually contains berries and nuts, may contain animal hair, undigested plant stems and roots

Activity: diurnal, nocturnal; often seen feeding during the day

Tracks: hind paw 7-9" (18-23 cm) long, 5" (13 cm) wide with 5 toes, turns inward slightly, looks like a human footprint, forepaw 4" (10 cm) long, 5" (13 cm) wide with 5 toes, claw marks on all feet; fore and hind prints are parallel, hind paws fall several inches in front of fore prints; shuffles feet when walking

Stan's Notes: Once seen across Georgia. Now localized to certain regions of the state. Unique to North America. Has a shuffling gait and frequently appears clumsy. It is not designed for speed, but can run up to 30 mph (48 km/h) for short distances. A powerful swimmer, however, and good at climbing trees. It has color vision, but poor eyesight and relies on smell to find most of its food. Often alone except for mating in early summer or when bears gather at a large food supply such as a garbage dump. Feeds heavily throughout summer, adding layers of fat for hibernation.

In northern parts of its range it hibernates up to five months per year starting in late fall. In Georgia it appears to hibernate for a much shorter time or not at all; occasionally wakes and moves around the den in winter. Heart rate drops from 70 to 10-20 beats per minute. Body temperature drops 1-12 °F (-17 to -11 °C), which is not enough to change mental functions. Does not eat, drink, defecate or urinate when hibernating despite rousing. A female can lose up to 40 percent of its body weight when hibernating.

A male has a large territory up to 15 square miles (39 sq. km) that often encompasses several female territories. Males fight each other for breeding rights and usually have scars from fights. They mature at 3-4 years, but don't become full size until 10-12 years. Males do not help to raise the young.

Females don't breed until 2-3 years of age. A female with more body fat when entering hibernation will have more cubs than others with less fat. If a female lacks enough fat, she will not give birth. Mothers average about 177 pounds (80 kg)–around 250 times the size of newborns. A short gestation and tiny cubs are the result of the reproductive process during hibernation.

cub

male

EXTIRPATED
no longer found

FORMER
RANGE

American Bison
Bison bison

Family: Goats, Sheep and Cattle (Bovidae)

Size: L 8-12' (2.4-3.7 m); T 12-19" (30-48 cm); H 5-6' (1.5-1.8 m)

Weight: M 1,000-2,000 lb. (450-900 kg); F 800-1,000 lb. (360-450 kg)

Description: Dark brown head, lighter brown body and large humped shoulders. Bearded with a long shaggy mane over head and shoulders. Long tuft-tipped tail. Both sexes have short curved horns, which are not shed.

Origin/Age: native; 20-25 years

Compare: A massive animal, difficult to confuse with any other. No longer roams freely in Georgia. Found only in managed areas such as private ranches.

Habitat: grasslands, open forests

Home: does not use a den or nest, even in bad weather or winter; beds in a different spot each night, rests in the open, laying on the ground

Food: herbivore; grasses and other green plants, lichens

Sounds: often quiet; male bellows during the rut, female snorts, young bawls for mother's attention

Breeding: Jul-Aug mating; 9-10 months gestation

Young: 1 calf every 1-2 years in May or June; born with reddish brown fur, stands within 30 minutes, walks within hours of its birth, joins herd at 2-3 days, acquires hump, horns and adult coloration at 2-3 months, weaned at 6-7 months

flehmening female

Signs: saucer-like depressions in dirt (wallows), 8-10' (2.4-3 m) wide, trees and shrubs with the bark rubbed off, shallow depressions in the grass are evidence of bison beds; scat is similar to that of the domestic cow, flat round patties, 12-14" (30-36 cm) wide

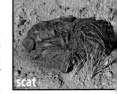

scat

Activity: crepuscular; often rests during the day to chew its cud

Tracks: front hoof 6-7" (15-18 cm) long, hind hoof slightly smaller, both with opposing crescents and more pointed in the front; hind hooves fall behind and slightly to the side of fore prints; crescents widen when walking in mud or running

Stan's Notes: The largest land mammal in North America and considered iconic to the New World. Sometimes called Buffalo, but not related to the Old World buffalo.

Historically, American Bison ranged across most of the United States and numbered in the tens of millions. Centuries ago, great herds would migrate long distances between summer and winter grounds. They were hunted to near extinction around the 1880s, when a government policy advocated extermination. By the early 1900s fewer than 1,000 bison remained in the country. Because bison are now kept behind fences in managed herds, they no longer migrate.

A gregarious animal, gathering in large herds of nearly 100 bison, mainly females (cows) and calves. Rolls and rubs itself in wallows to relieve insect bites.

Males (bulls) are usually found on their own or in a small group during fall and winter. A dominant bull will join a maternal herd late in summer before the rut. Cows mature at 2-3 years and stay fertile for about 24 hours. A bull will curl its upper lip and extend its neck (flehmening) when around cows, perhaps to detect estrus. Bulls "tend" cows that are entering estrus rather than maintaining harems.

Competing bulls strut near each other, showing off their large profile. Mature bulls occasionally face each other, charge, crash headfirst and use their massive necks to push each other. Sparring fights rarely result in injury. Sometimes goring or hooking occurs.

sparring

Atlantic Spotted Dolphin
Stenella frontalis

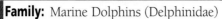

Family: Marine Dolphins (Delphinidae)

Size: L 6-6½' (1.8-2 m)

Weight: 250-275 lb. (113-124 kg)

Description: Smooth purplish gray body covered with white spots, especially on the sides. Nearly white belly. Often appears black from a distance. Short stocky snout (beak). Small round eyes on sides of head just behind the line of the jaw. Breathing hole on top of head behind eyes. Large fin on the back (dorsal) curves back and points toward the tail (falcate). Short, thick powerful tail. Long flippers. Some individuals have more spots than others. Male is longer and heavier than the female.

Origin/Age: native to waters off the coast of Georgia and the entire Atlantic Ocean; 20-25 years

Compare: Smaller than the Bottlenose Dolphin (pg. 303), which has shorter flippers and lacks white spots.

Habitat: open seas, deeper bays, inlets

Home: roams open waters with no well-defined territory, often following seasonal patterns; rests in open water near coral reefs

Food: ichthyophagous; fish, squid, invertebrates

Sounds: series of squeaks, whistles, chirps, growls, barks and chuckles above and below water

Breeding: Jun-Aug mating; 12 months gestation

Young: 1 calf every 2-3 years; born swimming, nurses for up to 1 year

mother and calf

Signs: shadows of large individuals swimming in groups of up to 50 individuals, riding bow waves of boats, feeding around fishing and shrimp boats, individuals breaking the surface of the water, leaping into the air or surfacing for air just offshore

Activity: diurnal, nocturnal; active year-round

Tracks: none

Stan's Notes: A small dolphin, often appearing very dark from a distance. Shows a large number of small white spots when seen up close. A congregation of spots results in a blaze or white stripe on the side. Amount of spots is highly variable among individuals.

Less common than the Bottlenose Dolphin (pg. 303). Doesn't do well in captivity and is not as familiar to the general public as the Bottlenose. Often in groups, known as pods or schools, of 10-20 dolphins; sometimes in larger groups of up to 50 individuals.

Occurring only in warm waters of the Atlantic, it is the second most common dolphin in the Gulf of Mexico. More common offshore than near shore, usually never closer than 5 miles (8 km) out. When near shore, it is thought to be responding to prey items heading toward shallow waters.

Has a smooth, streamlined body. Adults have 60-84 teeth. Young are born in spring and summer and lack spots. All ride the bow waves of large ships and jump out of the water.

The Delphinidae family has 33 species of dolphins and spouted whales, which are closely related. Dolphins and porpoises are very similar, but different. Both are air-breathing marine mammals, but the porpoise has a round head and lacks the beak (snout) of the dolphin. The dorsal fin on the back of the porpoise is small and triangular compared with the larger, swept-back dorsal fin of the dolphin. Because dolphins and porpoises are similar, their names are sometimes used interchangeably.

Bottlenose Dolphin

Tursiops truncatus

Family: Marine Dolphins (Delphinidae)

Size: L 8-8½' (2.4-2.6 m)

Weight: 450-550 lb. (203-248 kg)

Description: Smooth and streamlined gray body with a large head, short stocky snout (beak) and lighter belly. Small round eyes on the sides of head. Breathing hole on top of head behind the eyes. Large fin on the back (dorsal) curves back and points toward the tail (falcate). Short, thick powerful tail. Some individuals are darker than others. May have lighter areas of scarring from old injuries. Male is longer and heavier than the female.

Origin/Age: native to waters off the Georgia coast and the Atlantic and Pacific Oceans; 20-25 years

Compare: Atlantic Spotted Dolphin (pg. 299) is smaller, stockier and has white spots on its sides.

Habitat: open seas, bays, inlets, saltwater lagoons

Home: some stay in 1 bay, others roam open waters with no well-defined territory, often following seasonal patterns; rests in open water near coral reefs

Food: ichthyophagous; fish, squid, invertebrates

Sounds: series of squeaks, pops and chuckles above and below water

Breeding: Jun-Aug mating; 12 months gestation

Young: 1 calf every 2-3 years; born swimming, nurses for up to 1 year

breaching   pod

Signs: shadows of large individuals swimming in groups, riding bow waves of boats, feeding around fishing and shrimp boats, individuals breaking the surface of the water, leaping into the air (breaching) or surfacing for air just offshore

Activity: diurnal, nocturnal; active year-round

Tracks: none

Stan's Notes: A familiar marine mammal made famous by the television show, "Flipper." Now seen in many marine or aquarium displays and museums. The Bottlenose is the most widespread and common of coastal dolphins and can be seen in relatively shallow water in lagoons, bays and inlets. The majority, however, are found well out to sea. Found throughout the temperate and tropical waters of the world.

Often in groups, called pods or schools, of 2-20 individuals, but can be seen in larger groups of up to 100 dolphins. Some groups are sedentary, remaining in a small territory of one bay; others are migratory. Populations tend to increase off the coast of Georgia during fall and winter.

It is thought there are two distinct Bottlenose Dolphin forms in the Atlantic Ocean: inshore dolphins that inhabit shallow water and offshore populations remaining in deeper waters. Differences in body shape and fin size show that the inshore dolphins are adapting to shallower water.

Dolphins eat a wide variety of food depending on the abundance at the time. They eat mainly fish, including shark, tarpon, pike, rays, mullet, catfish and anchovies, along with eels. A dolphin can eat 40-50 pounds (18-23 kg) of food daily. Individuals of a group often work together when feeding. Sometimes several dolphins will herd fish into tight schools while others wait at the bottom and swim up to feed. Other times dolphins may simply chase fish into shallow water or onto beaches, where they lunge for their prey.

West Indian Manatee
Trichechus manatus

Family: Sea Cows (Trichechidae)

Size: L 10-15' (3-4.6 m)

Weight: 1,500-3,500 lb. (675-1,575 kg)

Description: An extremely large aquatic mammal. Uniformly gray overall with 2 front flippers and a large, wide round tail. Large blunt snout and tiny dark eyes. Large, flexible, prehensile upper lip, acting much like an elephant's trunk. Female is usually longer and heavier than the male.

Origin/Age: native; 50-70 years

Compare: No other extremely large mammal is found in the freshwater rivers of Georgia. Hard to confuse with any other mammal. Lacks the dorsal fin of the dolphins (pp. 299-303).

Habitat: freshwater rivers, around power plants discharging warm water, not ever far from the coast

Home: freshwater rivers (moves around seasonally), estuaries, coastal water

Food: herbivore; 60 species of aquatic plants, turtle grass, mangrove leaves, algae; also eats snails and other aquatic invertebrates that attach to plants; some individuals eat small amounts of small fish

Sounds: usually silent; can grunt and groan, exhales air audibly when surfacing

Breeding: any time of year; 12 months gestation

Young: 1 calf every 2-3 years; born swimming, with a weight of about 60 pounds (27 kg); nurses for up to 1 year; stays with the mother for up to 2 years

mother and calf

Signs: shadows of large individuals swimming in freshwater rivers, estuaries and coastal waters

Activity: diurnal, nocturnal; active year-round

Tracks: none

Stan's Notes: The origin of mermaid folklore. Also known as Sea Cow, Florida Manatee or Caribbean Manatee. Slow-moving, fully aquatic, placid animal that eats plants in shallow waters. Surfaces every 3-5 minutes for air; can stay underwater up to 15 minutes. Often travels alone or in small groups. Has been in Georgia for about 45 million years, according to fossil records.

Congregates in the warm springs of the Savannah River in winter, or at power plants that release warm water. Cannot survive water below 60 °F (16 °C). Disperses along the coast during summer, returning to Florida and Georgia rivers and estuaries for the winter. Able to survive in salt water, but needs fresh water to feed. Seen as far north as Cape Cod and New York City.

There are about 3,000 manatees in the United States. Considered an endangered species by the U.S. Fish and Wildlife Service. Adult numbers are decreasing and many predict that this species could become extinct in the not-so-distant future if population trends do not change. Because the manatee moves so slowly, its number one killer is speeding motorboats. Some individuals have up to 50 distinct scars from nearly fatal boat contacts.

A very long-lived animal and slow to reproduce. Females are known as cows, males are called bulls and young are calves. Like all mammals, manatee calves obtain nutrition from their mother's milk. Calves stay at their mother's side for the first few months and range farther away as they grow up.

The manatee has special nostrils with valves to keep out water. It lacks external ears, but hears well with internal ears. Mothers and calves make soft sounds to communicate with each other.

The manatee's upper lip is prehensile, dexterous, distantly related to an elephant's trunk and acts like a vacuum cleaner. Manatees use this lip to remove algae from the backs of other manatees.

GLOSSARY

Browse: Twigs, buds and leaves that deer and other animals eat.

Canid: A member of the Wolves, Foxes and Coyote family, which includes dogs.

Carnivore: An animal, such as a mink, fox or wolf, that eats the flesh of other animals for its main nutrition.

Carrion: Dead or decaying flesh. Carrion is a significant food source for many animal species.

Cecum: The large pouch that forms the beginning of the large intestine. Also known as the blind gut.

Cheek ruff: A gathering of long stiff hairs on each side of the face of an animal, ending in a downward point. Seen in bobcats.

Coprophagy: The act of reingesting fecal pellets. Coprophagy enables rabbits and hares to gain more nourishment since the pellets pass through the digestive system a second time.

Crepuscular: Active during the early morning and late evening hours as opposed to day or night. See *diurnal* and *nocturnal*.

Cud: Food regurgitated from the first stomach to the mouth, and chewed again. Cud is produced by hoofed animals such as deer or bison, which have a four-chambered stomach (ruminants).

Dewclaw: A nonfunctional (vestigial) digit on the feet of some animals, which does not touch the ground. Seen in deer.

Direct register: The act of a hind paw landing or registering in the track left by a forepaw, resulting in two prints that appear like one track. Usually occurs when walking.

Diurnal: Active during daylight hours as opposed to nighttime hours. Opposite of *nocturnal*.

Drey: The nest of a squirrel.

Duff: The layer of decaying leaves, grasses, twigs or branches, often several inches thick, on a forest floor or prairie.

Echolocation: A sensory system in bats, dolphins and some shrews, in which inaudible, high-pitched sounds are emitted and the returning echoes are interpreted to determine the direction and distance of objects such as prey.

Estrus: A state of sexual readiness in most female animals that immediately precedes ovulation, and the time when females are most receptive to mating. Also known as heat.

Extirpate: To hunt or trap into extinction in a region or state.

Flehmen: The lift of the upper lip and grimace an animal makes when it draws air into its mouth and over its Jacobson's organ, which is thought to help analyze the scents (pheromones) wafting in the air. Frequently seen in cats, deer and bison.

Fossorial: Well suited for burrowing or digging. Describes an animal such as a mole.

Gestation: Pregnancy. The period of development in the uterus of a mammal from conception up to birth.

Grizzled: Streaked or tipped with gray, or partly gray. Describes the appearance of some fur.

Guard hairs: The long outer hairs of an animal's coat, which provide warmth. Guard hairs are typically hollow and usually thicker and darker than the soft hairs underneath.

Haul out: A well-worn trail or area on the shore where an animal, such as an otter, climbs or hauls itself out of the water.

Herbivore: An animal, such as a rabbit or deer, that eats plants for its main nutrition.

Hibernation: A torpid or lethargic state characterized by decreased heart rate, respiration and body temperature, and occurring in close quarters for long periods during winter. See *torpor*.

Hoary: Partly white or silver streaked, or tipped with white or silver. Describes the appearance of some fur.

Hummock: A low mound or ridge of earth or plants.

Insectivore: An animal, such as a shrew, that eats insects as its main nutrition.

Keratin: A hard protein that is the chief component of the hair, nails, horns and hooves of an animal.

Microflora: Bacterial life living in the gut or first stomach of an animal. Microflora help break down food and aid in the digestive process.

Midden: A mound or deposit of pine cone parts and other refuse. A midden is evidence of a favorite feeding site of an animal such as a squirrel.

Morph: One of various distinct shapes, structural differences or colors of an animal. Color morphs do not change during the life of an animal.

Nictitating membrane: A second, inner eyelid, usually translucent, that protects and moistens the eye.

Nocturnal: Active during nighttime hours as opposed to daylight hours. Opposite of *diurnal*.

Nonretractile: That which cannot be drawn back or in. Describes the claws of a dog. Opposite of *retractile*.

Omnivore: An animal, such as a bear, that eats a wide range of foods including plants, insects and the flesh of other animals as its main nutrition.

Patagium: A thin membrane extending from the body to the front and hind limbs, forming a wing-like extension. Seen in flying squirrels and bats.

Population: All individuals of a species within a specific area.

Predator: An animal that hunts, kills and eats other animals. See *prey*.

Prey: An animal that is hunted, killed and eaten by a predator. See *predator*.

Retractile: That which can be drawn back or in. Describes the claws of a cat. Opposite of *nonretractile*.

Rut: An annually recurring condition of sexual readiness and reproductive activity in mammals, such as deer, that usually occurs in autumn. See *estrus*.

Scat: The fecal droppings of an animal.

Scent marking: A means of marking territory, signaling sexual availability or communicating an individual's identity. An animal scent marks with urine, feces or by secreting a tiny amount of odorous liquid from a gland, usually near the base of the tail, chin or feet, onto specific areas such as rocks, trees and stumps.

Semiprehensile: Suited for partially seizing, grasping or holding, especially by wrapping around an object, but not a means of full support. Describes the tail of an opossum.

Stride: In larger animals, the distance between individual tracks. In smaller animals, such as weasels, the distance between sets of tracks.

Subterranean: Below the surface of the earth.

Tannin: A bitter-tasting astringent found in the nuts of many plant species.

Torpor: A torpid or lethargic state resembling hibernation, characterized by decreased heart rate, respiration and body temperature, but usually shorter, lasting from a few hours to several days or weeks. See *hibernation*.

Tragus: A fleshy projection in the central part of the ear of most bats. The size and shape of the tragus may be used to help identify some bat species.

Tree rub: An area on small to medium trees where the bark has been scraped or stripped off. A tree rub is made by a male deer polishing his antlers in preparation for the rut.

Velvet: A soft, furry covering on antlers that contains many blood vessels, which support antler growth. Velvet is shed when antlers reach full size. Seen in the Deer family.

Vibrissae: Sensitive bristles and hairs, such as whiskers, that help an animal feel its way in the dark. Vibrissae are often on the face, legs and tail.

Wallow: A depression in the ground that is devoid of vegetation, where an animal, such as a bison, rolls around on its back to "bathe" in dirt.

HELPFUL RESOURCES

Emergency

For an animal bite, please seek medical attention at an emergency room or call 911. Injured or orphaned animals should be turned over to a licensed wildlife rehabilitator. Check your local listings for a rehabilitator near you.

Web Pages

The internet is a valuable place to learn more about mammals. You may find studying mammals on the net a fun way to discover additional information about them or to spend a long winter night. These web sites will assist you in your pursuit of mammals. If a web address doesn't work (they often change a bit), just enter the name of the group into a search engine to track down the new web address.

Site and Address:
Smithsonian Institution - North American Mammals
www.mnh.si.edu/mna

The American Society of Mammalogists
www.mammalsociety.org

National Wildlife Rehabilitators Association
www.nwrawildlife.org/home.asp

International Wildlife Rehabilitation Council
www.iwrc-online.org

Georgia Department of Natural Resources -
Wildlife Resources Division
www.georgiawildlife.com

Author Stan Tekiela's home page
www.naturesmart.com

Georgia's Artiodactyla Order

ORDER	SUBORDER	FAMILY	SUBFAMILY
Artiodactyla		Bovidae	Bovinae
		Cervidae	Capreolinae
			Cervinae
		Suidae	

Georgia's Carnivora Order

ORDER	SUBORDER	FAMILY	SUBFAMILY
Carnivora	Caniformia	Canidae	
		Mephitidae	
		Mustelidae	Lutrinae
			Mustelinae
		Procyonidae	Procyoninae
		Ursidae	Ursinae
	Feliformia	Felidae	Felinae

Even-toed Hooved Animals

American Bison pg. 295
Bison bison

White-tailed Deer pg. 287
Odocoileus virginianus

Fallow Deer pg. 283
Dama dama

Wild Hog pg. 279
Sus scrofa

Meat-eating Predators

Gray Fox pg. 255
Urocyon cinereoargenteus

Red Fox pg. 259
Vulpes vulpes

Coyote pg. 263
Canis latrans
Red Wolf pg. 267
Canis rufus

Eastern Spotted Skunk pg. 235
Spilogale putorius

Northern River Otter pg. 231
Lontra canadensis

Striped Skunk pg. 239
Mephitis mephitis

Least Weasel pg. 219
Mustela nivalis
Long-tailed Weasel pg. 223
Mustela frenata
Mink pg. 227
Mustela vison

Northern Raccoon pg. 251
Procyon lotor

Black Bear pg. 291
Ursus americanus

Bobcat pg. 271
Lynx rufus

Cougar pg. 275
Puma concolor

Box colors match the
corresponding section of the book.

Georgia's Cetacea Order

ORDER	SUBORDER	FAMILY	SUBFAMILY

| Cetacea | Odontoceti | **Delphinidae** | |

Georgia's Chiroptera Order

| | | **Molossidae** | Molossinae |

Chiroptera

| | Microchiroptera | **Vespertilionidae** | Vespertilioninae |

Dolphins

Atlantic Spotted Dolphin pg. 299
Stenella frontalis

Bottlenose Dolphin pg. 303
Tursiops truncatus

Bats

Brazilian Free-tailed Bat pg. 172
Tadarida brasiliensis

Little Brown Bat pg. 172
Myotis lucifugus
Eastern Small-footed Myotis pg. 172
Myotis leibii
Northern Myotis pg. 172
Myotis septentrionalis
Indiana Bat pg. 173
Myotis sodalis
Gray Myotis pg. 173
Myotis grisescens
Southeastern Bat pg. 173
Myotis austroriparius

Eastern Pipistrelle pg. 172
Pipistrellus subflavus

Evening Bat pg. 172
Nycticeius humeralis

Big Brown Bat pg. 169
Eptesicus fuscus

Silver-haired Bat pg. 173
Lasionycteris noctivagans

Eastern Red Bat pg. 173
Lasiurus borealis
Hoary Bat pg. 173
Lasiurus cinereus
Northern Yellow Bat pg. 173
Lasiurus intermedius
Seminole Bat pg. 173
Lasiurus seminolus

Rafinesque's Big-eared Bat pg. 173
Corynorhinus rafinesquii

Box colors match the
corresponding section of the book.

319

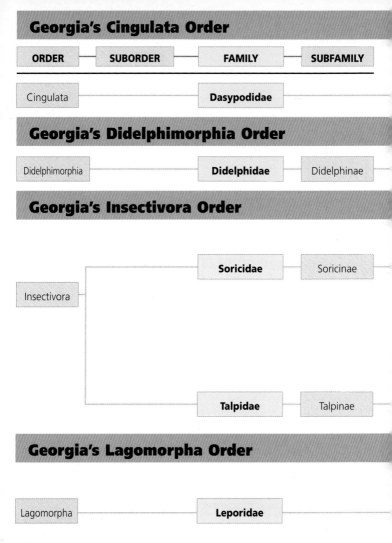

Georgia's Cingulata Order

ORDER	SUBORDER	FAMILY	SUBFAMILY

| Cingulata | | **Dasypodidae** | |

Georgia's Didelphimorphia Order

| Didelphimorphia | | **Didelphidae** | Didelphinae |

Georgia's Insectivora Order

| Insectivora | | **Soricidae** | Soricinae |
| | | **Talpidae** | Talpinae |

Georgia's Lagomorpha Order

| Lagomorpha | | **Leporidae** | |

Armadillo

Nine-banded Armadillo pg. 243
Dasypus novemcinctus

Marsupial

Virginia Opossum pg. 247
Didelphis virginiana

Shrews and Moles

Least Shrew pg. 37
Cryptotis parva

Masked Shrew pg. 41
Sorex cinereus
Pygmy Shrew pg. 45
Sorex hoyi
Smoky Shrew pg. 49
Sorex fumeus
Southeastern Shrew pg. 53
Sorex longirostris
Water Shrew pg. 65
Sorex palustris

Southern Short-tailed Shrew pg. 57
Blarina carolinensis
Northern Short-tailed Shrew pg. 61
Blarina brevicauda

Star-nosed Mole pg. 69
Condylura cristata

Eastern Mole pg. 73
Scalopus aquaticus

Hairy-tailed Mole pg. 77
Parascalops breweri

Rabbits

Marsh Rabbit pg. 203
Sylvilagus palustris
Appalachian Cottontail pg. 207
Sylvilagus obscurus
Eastern Cottontail pg. 211
Sylvilagus floridanus
Swamp Rabbit pg. 215
Sylvilagus aquaticus

Box colors match the
corresponding section of the book.

321

Georgia's Rodentia Order

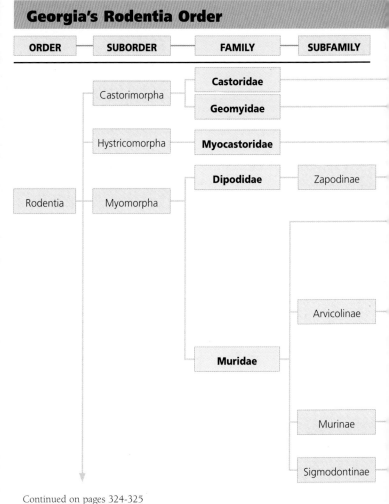

ORDER	SUBORDER	FAMILY	SUBFAMILY
	Castorimorpha	**Castoridae**	
		Geomyidae	
	Hystricomorpha	**Myocastoridae**	
Rodentia	Myomorpha	**Dipodidae**	Zapodinae
		Muridae	Arvicolinae
			Murinae
			Sigmodontinae

Continued on pages 324-325

Rodents

American Beaver pg. 165
Castor canadensis

Southeastern Pocket Gopher pg. 199
Geomys pinetis

Nutria pg. 161
Myocastor coypus

Meadow Jumping Mouse pg. 81
Zapus hudsonius

Woodland Jumping Mouse pg. 97
Napaeozapus insignis

Golden Mouse pg. 109
Ochrotomys nuttalli

Southern Red-backed Vole pg. 137
Clethrionomys gapperi

Woodland Vole pg. 141
Microtus pinetorum
Meadow Vole pg. 145
Microtus pennsylvanicus
Prairie Vole pg. 149
Microtus pennsylvanicus

Round-tailed Muskrat pg. 153
Neofiber alleni

Muskrat pg. 157
Ondatra zibethicus

House Mouse pg. 93
Mus musculus

Black Rat pg. 121
Rattus rattus
Norway Rat pg. 129
Rattus norvegicus

Eastern Harvest Mouse pg. 85
Reithrodontomys humulis

Oldfield Mouse pg. 89
Peromyscus polionotus
White-footed Mouse pg. 101
Peromyscus leucopus
Deer Mouse pg. 105
Peromyscus maniculatus
Cotton Mouse pg. 113
Peromyscus gossypinus

Marsh Rice Rat pg. 117
Oryzomys palustris

Hispid Cotton Rat pg. 125
Sigmodon hispidus

Eastern Woodrat pg. 133
Neotoma floridana

Box colors match the
corresponding section of the book.

Georgia's Rodentia Order *(continued)*

| ORDER | SUBORDER | FAMILY | SUBFAMILY |

Continued from pages 322-323

| Rodentia | Sciuromorpha | **Sciuridae** | Sciurinae |
| | | | Xerinae |

Georgia's Sirenia Order

| Sirenia | | **Trichechidae** | Trichechinae |

Rodents

Southern Flying Squirrel pg. 179
Glaucomys volans

Red Squirrel pg. 183
Tamiasciurus hudsonicus

Eastern Gray Squirrel pg. 187
Sciurus carolinensis

Fox Squirrel pg. 191
Sciurus niger

Eastern Chipmunk pg. 175
Tamias striatus

Woodchuck pg. 195
Marmota monax

Manatee

West Indian Manatee pg. 307
Trichechus manatus

Box colors match the
corresponding section of the book.

CHECK LIST/INDEX

Use the boxes to check the mammals you've seen.

PHOTO CREDITS

Dr. J. Scott Altenbach: 173 (Northern Yellow, Seminole)

Roger W. Barbour: 88, 134, 172 (Small-footed), 173 (Gray)

Rick and Nora Bowers: 106, 118, 124, 126, 172 (Brazilian), 216, 284 (all insets except scat)

Mary Clay/Dembinsky Photo Associates: 236 (main)

E. R. Degginger/Dembinsky Photo Associates: 38, 44, 70

Larry Ditto/KAC Productions: 280 (main)

Art Drauglis: 206, 208

Richard B. Forbes, Ph.D.: 162

Bill Klipp: 302

Gary Kramer: 280 (middle inset)

Dwight Kuhn: 64, 67 (both)

Barry Mansell: 110, 152, 154, 198, 200 (all)

Maslowski Productions: 36, 68, 82, 180 (main), 214, 218, 221 (top inset), 222, 225, 278, 280 (top and bottom insets)

Gary Meszaros/Dembinsky Photo Associates: 43 (top), 62, 146 (main), 147

Skip Moody/Dembinsky Photo Associates: 71

Philip Myers: 140

Stan Osolinski/Dembinsky Photo Associates: 224

Michael Palmer: 160

James F. Parnell: 43 (bottom inset), 90, 96, 220

Michael Patrikeev/Wild Nature Images: 48, 50, 76, 78

B. Moose Peterson, Wildlife Research Photography: 66

Ed Pivorun: 52, 54

Ann and Rob Simpson: 47, 56

Stan Tekiela: 40, 42, 46, 60, 72, 74 (all), 80, 92, 94 (both), 95, 100, 102, 103, 104, 116, 120, 122, 128, 130 (both) 136, 138, 144, 146 (inset), 148, 150 (inset), 156, 158 (all), 164, 166 (all), 168, 170 (inset), 172 (Little Brown, Northern), 173 (Silver-haired, Eastern Red, Hoary), 174, 176 (all), 178, 180 (both insets), 181, 182, 184 (all), 186, 188 (all), 189, 190, 192 (Sherman's, Eastern, black morph), 193, 194, 196 (all), 197, 202, 204, 210, 212 (all), 213, 226, 228 (all), 229, 230, 232 (all), 234, 236 (inset), 237, 238, 240 (all), 241, 242, 244 (all), 246, 248 (all), 249, 250, 252 (both), 253, 254, 256 (all), 257 (both), 258, 260 (all), 261 (both), 262, 264 (all), 265, 266, 268 (both insets), 270, 272 (all) 273, 274, 276 (all), 277, 282, 284 (main, scat), 286, 288 (all), 289, 290, 292 (all), 293, 294, 296 (all), 297, 304 (both)

Merlin D. Tuttle/Bat Conservation International, Inc.: 170 (main), 172 (Pipistrelle, Evening), 173 (Indiana, Southeastern, Rafinesque's)

John and Gloria Tveten: 39 (bottom inset), 132, 142, 150 (main)

John and Gloria Tveten/KAC Productions: 58, 84, 86, 108, 112, 114

R. Wayne VanDevender: 39 (top inset), 83, 98, 99, 221 (bottom inset)

Steve Williams: 298, 300

www.cameraview.com: 268 (main)

www.FloridaNaturePhotography.com: 192 (white morph)

www.oceangrant.com: 306, 308

ABOUT THE AUTHOR

Naturalist, wildlife photographer and writer Stan Tekiela is the originator of the popular state-specific field guides such as *Birds of Georgia Field Guide*. For over two decades, Stan has authored more than 100 field guides, nature appreciation books and wildlife audio CDs for nearly every state in the nation, presenting many species of birds, mammals, reptiles and amphibians, trees, wildflowers and cacti. Holding a Bachelor of Science degree in Natural History from the University of Minnesota and as an active professional naturalist for more than 20 years, Stan studies and photographs wildlife throughout the United States and has received various national and regional awards for his books and photographs. Also a well-known columnist and radio personality, his syndicated column appears in over 20 newspapers and his wildlife programs are broadcast on a number of Midwest radio stations. He is a member of the North American Nature Photography Association and Canon Professional Services. Stan resides in Victoria, Minnesota, with his wife, Katherine, and daughter, Abigail. He can be contacted via his web page at www.naturesmart.com.

T0125467